Disfellowshipped!
Forced Exile and Liberation.

Copyright © 2018 by Christopher L Hale

All rights reserved. Printed in the United States of America. No part of this book may be used or reproduced in any manner whatsoever without written permission except in the case of brief quotations embodied in critical articles or reviews.

This book is a work of non-fiction. However, names, characters, businesses, organizations, places, events, and incidents either are the product of the author's imagination or are used fictitiously. Any resemblance to actual persons, living or dead, events, or locales is entirely coincidental.

For information, email us:
info@freedomswitness.com

This Page Intentionally Left Blank

PROLOGUE

It is a cold Saturday morning. You and your wife are warmly nestled beneath a heavy layer of blankets. Your children are still sleeping soundly in their beds. It is your only day to sleep in and enjoy the comforts of your home, insulated from the freezing cold temperatures of the outdoors. A slight stir encourages you to bury yourself deeper into your blankets and snuggle up closer to your wife. Was that the sound of someone knocking on your door? You dismiss it. It is zero degrees outside with four feet of snow and ice everywhere. No one in their right mind would be out in this weather. Once again, slumber finds you. Suddenly the door chimes, and this time you are sure there is someone at your door. Since you are not expecting any visitors at ten in the morning on a Saturday, who could possibly be at your door? You guessed it.

Jehovah's Witnesses are a denomination distinct from mainstream Christianity. According to their 2014 Yearbook of Jehovah's Witnesses, as of August 2013, the organization reports a worldwide membership of nearly eight million.

Jehovah's Witnesses are best known for their door-to-door preaching, distributing literature such as *THE WATCHTOWER* and *AWAKE!*, refusing military service, and blood transfusions. They reject immortality of the soul, and hellfire, which they consider to be unscriptural doctrines. They consider secular society to be morally corrupt and under the influence of Satan, and most limit their social interaction to other Witnesses. Congregational disciplinary actions include *disfellowshipping*, a non-biblical term for formal expulsion and shunning. Baptized individuals who choose to leave on their own accord are considered *disassociated (italics)* and are also shunned.

Each year, more than seventy thousand members are disfellowshipped from this organization.

It is this unloving practice of disfellowshipping or shunning that has provoked me to tell my story. The practice of disfellowshipping and shunning members has caused much grief to those involved. Imagine completely cutting off someone you love simply because they no longer believe as you do or because they are removed from the religion in the name of discipline. This practice has destroyed countless lives and family relationships and has contributed to a number of suicides.

Four months ago, I was sitting in traffic near Chicago, thinking about nothing more than how badly I wanted to get home. As the traffic thickened, I noticed a long line of emergency vehicles coming toward me. While listening to the local news, I learned that a young man was threatening to jump from the bridge, and within minutes of that broadcast, he jumped to his death.

A short time later, I would learn that he was someone I knew very well. Recently disfellowshipped, having nowhere to turn, and with no effective way to deal with his grief, he took his own life. Jonathan was a humble young man, his spirit was loving and kind, and his knowledge of the Bible, deep. Jonathan was joyful and would welcome you to the Kingdom Hall as if he had known you his whole life. Jonathan would often comment during the meetings, always thought-provoking, never ever boring. Jonathan was a shining example for others in the congregation, me included. He was heavily engaged in the preaching work and believed with vigor the things he was taught.

However, Jonathan was a thinker and even dedicated a full year of his life as a volunteer at WATCHTOWER headquarters. His entire life was centered on following and reasoning upon the scriptures as they were taught to him to disprove any dissenting thought. Jonathan had little experience with any secular thought outside of WATCHTOWER's way of thinking. So, when his thoughts were challenged by other deep thinkers on the validity of WATCHTOWER teachings, and he could not disprove their assertions, he approached the elders with his questions. As you can imagine, they could not answer his questions either, and subsequently, they disfellowshipped him for apostasy. In other words, they expelled him for being a thinker.

Jonathan had become a shattered believer. A man abandoned by his family and friends for daring to question, daring to seek the truth. While it is important not to negate the severity of his desperation, it also underscores the importance to break free from such control, finding and living our own truth.

In my journey of recovery, I have encountered many stories similar to this. Many of you who have been disassociated or have been disfellowshipped have been suffering on a level that many find hard to imagine. Essentially, this person is being cut off from family and friends for reasons that would seem to the average person as trivial. Our lives on this earth can be full of joyful times and hard times, and we need to share those moments with the people closest to us, this is how we cope and grow. It is unfair to single out just the

WATCHTOWER Society for, in fact, religion as an institution has destroyed millions of families using fear and coercion to their own ends. It is time to recognize the fear in ourselves and around us, conquer it, and take our control back. Religion is not about a belief in God necessarily, in my opinion. Religion is about a structured set of doctrines and rules to keep a group of people acting in one accord. Religion is about fear and conformity. Along my journey, I have developed my personal belief system based on my own reasoning. I believe it is the right of each person on this earth to have the same. The work of reasoning is not an easy task. It requires deliberation and a willingness to accept conflicting views until one or many become balanced with your mental, emotional, and psychological self.

Part of my journey has led me to the personal conclusion that there is no God in the traditional sense which is taught by most Christian churches. But I realize that many of the people that may be reading my memoir may have strong beliefs that are God-centric. For this reason, I reference God many times as a means to help tell the story. In my opinion, there is no clear way to know what the essence of God really is, although the Bible says that we are created in his image. Without an explicit manifestation for my eyes, I am forced to think of God as something or someone more abstract. Could 'God' be the collective universe with all its galaxies, stars, suns, and worm holes? Could 'God' be a collective of everything around us that lives and breathes, including humans themselves?

The debate about the origin of life rages on and on. But when I considered the religious insistence that a 'man like God' created human life and the universal ecosystem but then has been notably absent in some of the most horrific events in the history of mankind, I had to do a hard reset. I had to put my fears aside and step into the unknown.

DISFELLOWSHIPPED! Forced Exile and Liberation

CHAPTER 1

It was the nightmare from which I thought I would never awaken. Just another bad dream that I hoped would end with the dawning of a new day and the burst of the morning sunlight. I would spend the next six years living in a dream-like state as if watching my life in a bad film being unable or unwilling to change the channel. By now, you must be wondering what sort of movies I was watching before bed. Most people have nightmares and dreams as a result of some fear, for example, a fear of drowning. Others dream of the day's events, future events or something they may have seen on television. While the foregoing might be good reasons for a nightmare, mine were quite different. You see, my worst dream had come true.

I had been disfellowshipped.

Let me explain who I have become by starting at the beginning.

The year was early 1969, and my mother, a very young and tender nineteen-year-old was heavy with child, me. According to her story, she got a knock on the door from a young blonde haired and eager Jehovah's Witness. What ensued was a flurry of promises that her firstborn child would never have to deal with the pains of life in this world. That this child would more than likely never graduate high school and that college would be a cost she and my father need not be concerned with. Why? Because the paradise, the New System, as Jehovah's Witnesses called it, was "right around the corner." Of course, this mother-to-be accepted this message with an open heart. She was newly married and dealing with the challenges that came with starting a new family. Intrigued, she accepted a Bible study and the chance to receive everlasting life on a paradise earth if she would be good enough.

Since I am currently being shunned by both of my parents, I have to rely on my own recollection for the earlier details of my life growing up in this religion. I can recall that my earliest experience of being one of Jehovah's Witness was not an overwhelming one until my father was converted. Eventually, there would be four of us children, two boys and two girls, and I was the oldest. We would all become heavily exposed to the doctrines of Jehovah's Witnesses long before our teenage years.

My mother was easy going and grew up as an only child. Her father was not very active in her life which may explain why she married at such a young age. From my earliest days, I took note of the lackluster relationship between my mother and hers. Since she grew up without any siblings, it seemed to me at times that we were there to provide something so natural that she missed out on by not having any brothers or sisters of her own.

She took great pride in us as children. She encouraged us to spend time with each other first before inviting the neighbors. As a result of this, we were all very close as children, we rode bikes and explored our summers together. We were each other's best friends, and that could not have made my mother happier. I can still remember when I was about six years old, the care my mother took in getting us dressed for school, making sure we were all buttoned up to be dropped off at school or whatever activity we were to be involved with.

As an adult man with children of my own, I fully understand the appeal of the religion and its promises. About the time I was born, the word was awash in civil and racial unrest. I am quite certain that my black parents back then had to suffer through blatant racism laced with vulgar speech and periodic violence. I can imagine the instability of that environment, black people everywhere marching and fighting for rights that we have come to commonly expect today. I am sure she wondered endlessly about the future of her two children, and it probably gave her no small amount of anxiety. My mother did what good mothers always do; she did what she believed was best for her children at the time.

I remember going to the Kingdom Hall, how nice everyone was, and the old ladies who would always give me candy for sitting through the boring meetings with hours of mindless dribble coming from the stage. I cannot say it was unbearable because I knew at the end that Sister Carter always had that brown lunch bag full of candy. I could stick my hand into that bag with the full expectation that my hand would come back with a fist full of creamy delights. Sister Carter—I remember her so well. A chunky white woman with pale blue hair and a very warm smile that did not seem to notice that I was only being nice to her because of the brown lunch bag that held my creamy delights. Perhaps she knew. Perhaps she knew that the only reason I could endure the dribble coming from the stage was those creamy delights she held for me in that paper bag.

I only knew her as Sister Carter, but I knew her husband as Charlie, Charlie Carter. The coolest old dude I had ever met in my life. I admired Brother Carter. He always called me "little buddy" as his white hair cropped head shook when he said those words. Was that a part of his swagger? He was super cool, always sporting a cutting edge tie clip and collar pin. His suits? Usually a light beige or electric blue. He had a bow-legged walk, like a real pimp. Now that I think about it, I think Brother Carter had a thing for the "sistas," if you know what I mean. He was a "brotha" kind of cool. Whenever Brother Carter was called to the stage for a special announcement or to give a sermon, I paid special attention. After all, he was married to the candy lady, and I understood his influence.

Perhaps the coolest thing about Brother Carter was his Caddies. This man had more Cadillacs in his garage than anyone I had known at this point in my life. How was this possible? Was he a real pimp? I could imagine Brother Carter sitting in his Caddy, smoking a cigar behind dark windows while he pimped his bitches out for that candy money. Actually, this description aptly describes our Saturday morning field service ministry outing. Every Saturday morning, my mother would bring us to the Kingdom Hall to get ready for a morning of door knocking and boorish presentations of the WATCHTOWER and AWAKE! magazines. Brother Carter would assign territory maps to the different car groups and send them into the 'field' to get the morning ministry started. As I said early, I think that Brother Carter was a pimp. He would drive around the streets for half an hour dropping the sisters off on different street corners. He would drive around and talk to the other pimps (car group leaders) and later return to that same corner to pick them up. When we were done with our door knocking, they would always give him money. Charles Carter was more than an elder, more than a husband to the candy lady, and more than just an old man, he was the Cadillac Pimp. It was my goal each and every Saturday morning to make sure I was in the car group with Brother Carter. I was his boy. Despite my father being violently opposed, he took it upon himself to make sure I was indoctrinated the right way.

Jehovah's Witnesses are adept and highly skilled at using fear tactics. In the family relationship where either the husband or wife was opposed to the other's decision to become a Jehovah's Witness, they were said to be violently opposed. Many stories were told about spouses destroying literature, hiding car keys, husbands forbidding wives to attend meetings, and so on. Stories such as these served to unite the followers and confirm the fact they MUST be the true religion because the Devil is using their spouses to keep them from entering paradise.

I do not recall my father being violently opposed to anything, except when he was drunk. He might break a few things but never make any real strong efforts to keep my mother from attending the meetings several nights a week. Actually, he may have viewed it more like a few hours of uninterrupted freedom to do whatever he wanted. Brother Carter was a frequent visitor at our house, always trying to interest my father in a Bible discussion. In between his beer chugging and cigarette smoking, I thought there would be no chance. I might as well start looking for a new father, as this one would die in Armageddon. This was God's Great War against the wicked people living on the earth; especially those who are not Jehovah's Witnesses.

From the outside looking in, my father was a decent man. He was a particularly handsome guy who held a steady job. We lived in a decent neighborhood. I do not recall any utilities ever being turned off or there not being enough food to eat. My Dad went to work each and every day, worked hard, and it seemed as if we took vacations every year. There were things that I noticed in those early days when I was between ages eight to fourteen. I knew that my mom and dad had some problems. Sometimes he would drink too much and engage in late night excursions to some local bar where he would flirt with fairly unattractive women. I knew things were a little off when he would come home in the middle of the night smelling like beer and stale cigarettes, wake me up, and make me talk to him about 'guy stuff'. He was gone a lot during the week and often came home late at night, or sometimes he "worked" nights. We did not care that much because he always made it up to us on Friday nights with Pizza and scary late night television shows. Saturday morning would continue the fun as he would sometimes watch cartoons with us and clown around acting out roles as Superman, Batman or sometimes even Wonder Woman.

But, I knew my dad had some issues. He was a man to be feared, especially with that belt in hand. But he was, for all his faults, a fun dad. But all of that was about to change as if overnight.

Going to the Kingdom Hall was like going to a social event. I made a few good friends and learned to socialize with people of all different races and ages. Even knocking on doors and giving presentations was not all that bad, and I would dare say that we may have liked it a little bit. My mother made it tolerable for us kids. The meetings were long and somewhat tedious. My mother knew that we needed to have variety in our lives and made quite a bit of effort to give that to us. Can you imagine getting dressed up every Saturday morning and knocking on door after door in extreme weather conditions only to have most people tell you to get lost? After two to three hours of this, my mother would show her appreciation by taking us for ice cream. Can you imagine the feeling we had when after spending hours in the ministry knocking on people's doors, telling them our truth, judging them, condemning them for not worshipping our God and feeling content, we ate ice cream? We were saving lives; we deserved our ice cream.

What could be better?

At the time, I thought that our little paradise could only get better if our beer drinking, cigarette smoking, fun time father would become a witness. Oh, how great our lives would be! It was then that I, the most influential of the children, began a relentless campaign to get my father to come to the 'side of the truth'. I was the perfect ambassador and recruiter for the WATCHTOWER Bible and Tract Society. I had fully accepted the indoctrination not because it appealed to my young intellect, but out of fear. Armageddon was probably the biggest and scariest word I knew how to spell at twelve years old. The word inspired fears of a fiery death in my mind and colored my daily thoughts and dreams. So, I figured if I were this scared of 'Armageddon', then perhaps my dad would be too. I can remember sitting in the Kingdom Hall and hearing time and time again about all the things that did not meet with Jehovah's approval. There were so many things that I often wondered if there was anything that he actually did approve of.

I knew that Jehovah did not approve of smoking. There were fantastic stories about life long smokers who miraculously gave up smoking when they started studying with Jehovah's Witnesses and learned that God disapproved of smoking. The funny thing is, I could never find anything in the bible that forbade smoking cigarettes, cigars or even weed. Well, it did not matter if it was in the Bible explicitly or not. It was in the WATCHTOWER. The

WATCHTOWER leaders, the governing body members, were the mouthpiece of Jehovah himself. It was made known that smoking was bad, and those who smoked would not survive Armageddon.

So, armed with this factual information, I just had to save my father. I had to save him and my 'Grandma Chimney', who also was a heavy smoker, from Armageddon, which was "just around the corner." Out of the two living grandmothers, my 'Grandma Chimney' was my favorite. Looking back, I realize that she was probably hostile to Jehovah's Witnesses when they kicked on her door and for a good reason. However, to us, she was as sweet as she was sneaky. She understood that children should not be denied Christmas presents when they are young, and so she would invite us over a few days after Christmas and give us gifts. Since she was not giving on Christmas Day, my parents felt this was acceptable. The same rule applied to birthdays.

Often times on a boring weekend, we would beg our parents to take us to 'Grandma Chimney's' house and often my parents would remind my sister and me to always be aware of opportunities to preach to grandma. I do not remember having any doctrinally intelligent conversations with my grandmother, but I do recall telling her that she would "die at Armageddon" if she did not attend the Kingdom Hall with us. I do not remember if she laughed at us, but I do know that she felt sad for us.

My grandmother eventually stopped smoking, but it had nothing to do with my Armageddon death threats; she did it for health reasons and died a happy and satisfied Baptist.

Good thing I did not save her. My father, on the other hand, would not be so lucky.

For as many that had tried to start a Bible study with my father, Brother Carter would be the winner. He seemed to be the perfect choice, my father respected him for some reason, and I think his wife was secretly in love with my dad's chocolate complexion—she was forever baking him cherry pies.

As odd as this may seem, I do not remember his baptism as well as I can remember all the physical abuses that came as a result of me not wanting to conform to all the ridiculous demands of a Jehovah Witness father, hell-bent on making his already well-mannered family into WATCHTOWER robots. I vividly recall the announcement at the Kingdom Hall welcoming a new brother to the congregation, my father. I was proud because I thought I had saved his life, but in reality, I had taken steps toward destroying my own. He became very popular very quickly. An excellent speaker and with a charisma I had not seen before in him, he quickly became a leader. People in the congregation looked up to him and very soon many were leaning upon him for his sage advice, relying on his ability to use scripture to advise their situation. It was kind of cool having a father that was always being called on to offer prayer and to give talks from the stage, often delivering some of the lighter 'special needs' programs. Special Needs programs are delivered to the pew sitters when the elders decide that a particular trend may have a negative effect on the congregation and must be addressed. For example, a 'special needs' program could be about the prevalence of sisters wearing skirts above the knee and yoga pants or maybe even the brothers wearing tight fitting suits and workout clothes. I often enjoyed the opportunity to see some leg at the weekly meetings. In those days, you were pretty lucky if you could get some elbow action.

My father was baptized now and, by WATCHTOWER standards, doing very well. I looked up to him and wanted to make sure I did nothing to make him look bad.

Then he became an elder. I can remember being somewhat proud to be in the club, the son of an Elder club. This new status carried with it a sense of superiority even if it were only by association. Looking back, I may have even thought his new status afforded me a level of protection from prosecution for certain offenses. It seemed that other children of Elders got away with murder. Jehovah's Witnesses were then and still are today also famous for skate parties. This involved renting out the whole skating rink so that we can have good clean and wholesome fun without having any association with worldly non-believers. These skate parties were always chaperoned by a few Elders and were tightly controlled. The music was audited, and skating too close to another female with the lights down low was not going to happen—quite ridiculous looking back on it. However, there were always those few kids that managed to skirt the rules; hell, they could totally bend them out of whack. These were the elite, the children of Elders.

Many times after having been bored to death with the tightly controlled skate party and IF you had a car and IF your father was an elder, you MIGHT get invited to the after-party at someone's house where all the real fun could take place. There would always be someone there with the mix-tape, the music that was normally off limits along with some beer and, of course, there would be girls. You know, the ones that would never let themselves be seen as indecent in their dress or conduct at the Kingdom Hall? Most of the skate parties I attended were always north of where I grew up and mostly populated by Caucasian congregations, where most of the trouble seemed to be.

I grew up on the East side of town where most of the congregations were primarily African American, most of the Elders were black and in many cases very staunch in how they handled their position—their privilege as it was then called. It was important to keep your family in line to at least look like you were presiding over your family in a kingly manner. This meant that no one in your family was to question your authority, nor act in a way that was contrary to what was expected. Many of these elders had little else in the way of worldly responsibilities, meaning that most of them held menial positions and jobs with no possibilities of upward mobility. Being an Elder afforded them the opportunity to be someone, to enjoy a title, to have and use authority. Elders in the black Jehovah Witness community did not take any flack from anyone, especially not from their family. The position and the ego were too important; public perception before family, always.

However, things seemed different when you got outside of the black Jehovah Witness community. While the Caucasian Elders took their responsibilities seriously, they did not seem to go overboard with their authority. In my own personal experience, I had the most fun with the children of Elders from the West and North side, and they were the ones that should have gotten into the most trouble, but did not. But as I would learn later, these Elders were more interested in keeping their families together and maintaining their cohesion rather than exposing their dirty laundry to the view of the entire Jehovah Witness community. In other words, they protected their families from the public scrutiny of the judicial committees.

If I ever thought I would get some protections from my newly minted Elder father, I would be mistaken.

Becoming an elder was like reaching celebrity status. You now have a following. You have people that will now hang onto every word or piece of advice you offer. Being appointed to serve as an elder is akin to being promoted in your job. New title gives you a new air of respectability. You are somebody now. You can make decisions, and you now have the right to make declarations and demands on people without anyone really challenging you, at least not in public. You are an elder now. The governing body, a group of men responsible for the day-to-day operations of the religion, has given you authority to execute their commandments upon others and to carry out his orders knowing that most will be followed without question. A solid prescription for success in the WATCHTOWER organization is to follow without question. I never figured my father to be one of those types, but in retrospect, I now see that he was. He put his thinking on hold in order to succeed and to be a somebody, to be an elder, to have followers. He wanted to be the chief administrator of the robot army. One of the requirements for being an elder and maintaining that status was that your family had to act in lockstep; they had to show that the robotic indoctrination had taken hold. My dad, the just-appointed elder together with his newly christened authority, thought he could practice and perfect the robotic indoctrination techniques on his family.

He was wrong. My mother would constantly remind him that although he was the head of the family, she was the "neck that turned the head." What she meant was that he was not to make all the decisions about the family's future on his own. She was to be consulted. But because my father's eldership relied heavily on how his family was perceived by others in the congregation and to protect his position of authority and the perception he carried amongst members of the group, he became a tyrant.

While my father's tyranny hurt all members of the family, I would for many years suffer physical and emotional abuse far worse than anything inflicted upon my siblings.

To be fair, my father was not an inherently evil man. He was not unkind, mean or selfish, at least not initially. As I mentioned earlier, he was quite dutiful in the way he cared for his family. It is fair to say that I did not really know him well in my early years. My father was not a man of feelings, not one to give compliments or share his intimate thoughts, but yet not without emotion, primarily anger. He would not tolerate any disobedience out of any of his children of the time, especially my sister and me, although I think all my siblings would agree that I bore the brunt of his displeasure the majority of the time. For many years after my father became a witness, I lived in fear. Always looking over my shoulder for the next time I might get a whipping with his belt, many times not looking forward to coming home from school. My father's motto was "beat first and ask questions later." It was important that the first born be bought into strict obedience such that no command given by him could be ignored or even questioned. Interestingly, this sort of physical discipline would prepare me well for the mental and emotional enslavement I would suffer as one of Jehovah's Witnesses for years to come.

My father quickly removed my sister and me from all "worldly extracurricular activities" that might interfere with our theocratic captivities like attending the Kingdom Hall for seven meetings per week, ministry on the weekend, and the countless family and personal study events we had at home. This incredibly tight schedule did not leave much time for us to do things we really wanted to do as kids. Oh, how we hated the family study. I recall one instance when I had purchased with my allowance, some extra fly dress shoes for myself. I boldly wore them to the family study knowing that my father would make an issue with it since he told me not to buy them because I was to be "no part of the world." Well, at some point during our study, he asked me if I thought buying those shoes was being like the world or no part of the world. I told my dad that they were "just stinking shoes." Keep in mind I was fourteen at the time. Instead of trying to determine my intentions, he threw his heavy briefcase at me and my shoes in the trash.

A simple conversation with me would have revealed that I was trying to impress a girl at the Kingdom Hall.

My father never understood me as a teen. Had he forgotten that he was at one time my age? Did he forget that teenagers start to develop their own interests and tastes as they get older? I hated wearing the same suit over and over again to all the meetings and in field service. My dad made more money than most in our congregations, but in his die hard attempts to make humble the fourteen-year-old, I hardly got any new clothes. I was the brunt of jokes from all the other young boys in the Kingdom Hall. My suit jacket was three or four inches below my elbow, and my pants were highwaters. Remember that, high-waters? I was embarrassed to leave my seat during the meetings. I would wait till everyone else left, and then I would go to the car. One suit, one tie, one shirt and ragged ass shoes. It seemed to me that the other young witness boys looked forward to coming to the Kingdom Hall so that they could tease me.

Growing up in this religion, I really had no genuine friends. Dad's main goal, it seemed, was to make us the family that no one wanted to be around. It appeared at the time that we were never invited to anyone's house to play and missed out on most of the fun things going on in our congregation. It felt like our family was on the "no invite" list. My mother had to beg other parents to let her kids be part of their activities. I never quite understood why the other children did not like us. Maybe we were perceived as weird because we looked and acted so differently than even the "normal" Witness kids. No one knew the sort of torture we endured under the tyrannical rule of my father. Can you imagine being sent to your bedroom after family study with no dinner because you did not know the answers to bullshit questions that you could not comprehend at fourteen years of age? Who wants to sit and study the Bible for two to four hours on Saturday afternoon while all the neighborhood kids are outside playing?

Anyone that did not believe as Jehovah's Witnesses did was considered worldly and "bad association that could spoil useful habits." Every effort was made by families to make sure that they did not manifest any earthly traits or desire for worldly things. They taught that true Christians had to be separate from the world of unbelieving heathens. For a teenager, other than home, there was no place of greater influence than school. Before my father became an active nutcase Witness, I was a very energetic kid. I played team sports and was starting to show some promise on the track team. I played clarinet and was learning percussion and signed up to learn every musical genre the school had to offer at the time. I was really starting to develop some appreciation for classical jazz, but my all-time favorite was the marching band. There was nothing like football season in high school. I was never going to be big enough or bad enough to play on the team, but I was good enough to play in the band. Being on the field for the pre-game and half-time shows gave me a sense of pride and accomplishment beyond anything I had ever felt. Every kid wants to be admired for some talent, for something they can do well. They want to be admired by their parents, their friends, and especially, the girls.

I was doing it. I was in the marching band. I was making friends and being invited to hang out at the local pizza shop after the games. My music teacher really liked me because I showed up and gave it all my effort. There were cheerleaders. I looked forward to the half-time show because there was always a pretty girl that wanted to hold hands with the drummer.

But, I was showing signs of worldliness, according to WATCHTOWER policies. I had to be reined in. When would I have enough time to save people from Armageddon if I were busy learning how to play musical instruments and participating in school athletics? Something would have to change, so my father pulled my sister, who was learning how to play the flute at the time, and me from all of our extracurricular 'worldly' activities—or so he thought.

For some reason, I do not recall what my sister did, but I did not follow his orders. I did not quit. Although I was forced to withdraw from the marching band because most of the games were on Friday night during our family study time, I managed to stay enrolled for a complete school year in numerous other music genre classes. However, this secret would not last forever.

One day, my dad got a call from my principal when I was a freshman in high school. The principal reported that a student in my music class had accused me of stealing his drumsticks, and of course, I had denied it. After all, I had a collection of drumsticks in my locker; it was what I spent my monthly allowance on. Each month when dad gave us money for performing chores, I would ride my bike to my favorite music store and haggle for the best price for premium drumsticks. My sticks were everything, the connection to my interests, my love of drumming, and maybe a career in a well-known rock band, who knows.

But on that day, I was a drumstick thief. As I walked home from school, I was so gripped with fear that I actually started to believe that I had stolen the drumsticks just so I could be prepared for the whipping when I got home. However, nothing I could do or say would prepare me for what lay ahead.

I hate recliners. I will not sit in one, I will not own one, and I will not have one in my house or any place I choose to live. I hate the look and especially the feel of them. I will sit on the floor before I opt to sit in a recliner. It is not even a love-hate relationship; I just hate recliners. What did a recliner ever do to me to merit such scorn? Nothing really but be an unwilling pawn in my father's evil ploy to destroy me. Well, maybe not destroy but discipline for sure.

My father had a recliner; in fact, he had two recliners. The first pair was made of a blue velvet-like material, very soft to the touch. I was very excited about our first pair of recliners. They were purchased with my father's comfort in mind, and we were rarely allowed to sit in them. There were times when we knew that dad was not coming home for the evening, and we would sit in the recliners, kings and queens if even for a moment. My dad always preferred the recliner closest to the wall away from the front door, and we would often find him there sleeping after a long day at work. Over time, we noticed that the chair was beginning to lose its luster and freshness, and slowly that old-dad-who-believes-in-showers-twice-per-week-to-keep-the-water-bill-down smell took over.

The recliner smelled like old black ass.

Then one day, as I returned home from school, I noticed the blue velvet recliners were gone, both of them. Evidently, new furniture was on the horizon. That's exciting, I thought. New recliners? Lord, please let them be leather this time. As I started walking up the driveway, I noticed that one of the recliners was sitting on the curb awaiting trash pickup day and that the material had been torn from it. Add to this, my dad was home early. I stopped for a moment to look at the broken down recliner, to examine its anatomy of sorts. How exactly does a recliner recline? I looked for the reclining lever and paid close attention to the simple gear-like mechanisms that work in perfect synch with each other to perform the reclining action and wondered what bright engineer had dreamed this up and if he was rich by now. Of particular interest to me was the actual rocker glide itself. It was unlike what you find on an average rocking chair. This one was shaped like a sine wave. I noticed that this essential piece of the recliner's rocking mechanism was broken off from the rest of the chair. It is all trash anyway, and I made my way into the house to see what sort of pain was coming my way.

On an average day, I would walk into the living room and would see dad sitting in that blue recliner. Either he was studying Jehovah's Witness shit or doing a crossword puzzle, he always had a furrowed brow or a frown. Did he hate reading the Jehovah Witness bullshit as much as I did or was he deep in thought trying to convince himself that the lies were true? I hated seeing him in that recliner. Sitting there pretending not to hear and not to see. This man, looking at me, watching me, judging me.

But at that moment, he was just standing there, for me, no point of reference for there was no blue recliner. Why was he standing there? What the hell is your problem, man, I whispered as if my mind was standing next to me.

"Your music teacher called," he said.
"So?"—did I just say that?

"Your music teacher says you stole Michael's drumsticks from his locker," he snorted.
"No, I didn't, and I don't know what you are talking about."
My mother was standing close by in the kitchen; she was trying her best not to get involved. At this point, my sister walks in the house moments behind me. He directs her to go upstairs to get started on her homework as we needed to be at the Kingdom Hall by seven in the evening.
"I am so sick and tired of you telling lies all the time. I want the truth, or you are going to regret it," he shouted.
"I'm telling you the truth. I didn't steal this boy's drumsticks. I have my own, plenty of them."
At that moment, I pulled out my own sticks and showed them. He took them from me and disappeared outside. Still trembling from fear, I figured I had dodged a bullet. Moments later, he came back in with something large and wooden in his hands, my eyes were unbelieving.

Why was he standing in the living room shouting at me with the sine wave shaped rocker from the broken down recliner in his hand?

"If you are not going to tell me the truth, I will beat it out of you," he shouted.
He then proceeded to ask me several more times the same lame ass question.
And I gave him the same honest and truthful answer. This would not do any longer, so he made

me put my hands on the piano that loomed large in our small living room. He then proceeded to whack me with all his manly strength on my butt with that sine wave shaped wooden rocker while he kept asking the same thing: "Did you steal the drumsticks?"

"No, I did not!" I screamed. WHACK! The beating repeated over and over until I passed out on the floor.

As I lay on the floor slowly regaining consciousness, the monster was speaking, yelling, asking more questions.

Did I just hear this man tell my mother to get a bucket of water? Reality was a cold splash in the face as I lay on the floor of our tiny living room, at that point, feeling no pain. "Get up," says the asshole. "Hands on the piano." More questions. WHACK! I feel nothing. More questions, same answer. WHACK! No more tears. I was numb. It seemed like an hour had passed when my mother finally stepped up out of pure shame and said, "ENOUGH." My frustrated father threw down his weapon, stomped up the stairs, and leaned over the rails. "Next time you lie to me, I will beat you to death with a baseball bat." At that moment, I was certainly powerless to understand or even comprehend what this could mean for me, unable to imagine that things could ever get any worse. But now, as an adult and confronting the pure knowledge of the abuse I suffered at his hands, beating me with a baseball bat would probably have killed me.

Then he went on to the Kingdom Hall.

Mom prepared a bath of Epsom salt for me. That is where I spent my evening. I had open gashes of flesh on my ass. It was bleeding and swollen to where I could not even fit into my pajamas. The next morning, my mother sent me to school with a note: **Please allow my son to stand during class. He is suffering from lower back pain.** Later that day, my music teacher apologized to me for his mistake. Michael had left his drumsticks out on the practice field.

My father was not an inherently evil man. The 'TRUTH', the theories, and the religious indoctrinations of the Jehovah's Witnesses made him into an evil psychopath.

The next years would be filled with similar experiences although none would be quite as violent, but abusive nonetheless. As I continued through my high school years, I had many experiences both good and bad but very typical of the teenage years. All the kids around me were making college plans. Where are you going to college? They would often ask. Too embarrassed to tell them that I was not allowed to pursue a college career, I told them I was going to Ohio State. What will you study? Where will you be staying, on campus? Did you get a scholarship? Did your parents go to college? What were their majors? Have you thought about going to a Historically Black College or University (HBCU)? Do you want to be my roommate?

No, I could not tell them that my parents wanted me to go to WATCHTOWER headquarters and work in the factory printing books for the rest of my life, or walk door to door for ninety hours a month (pioneering) peddling these books.

I actually had the balls to tell my dad that I was going to college. His response and I quote: "The only way you can live under this roof is if you pioneer."

So, feeling defeated and without the will to do something different, I would waste the next twenty-seven years of my life living a lie.

Jehovah's Witnesses are strongly encouraged not to marry outside of their religion. When I was younger and looking for a potential marriage mate, I—like so many others—thought the primary reason behind this was to keep us firmly grounded in our religious foundation. But in reality, I believe it was to limit or discourage thinking or reasoning along different lines. By controlling one's ability to reason and compare, the organization keeps their numbers high because its members believe they are the only ones with the way to salvation. Let's consider this for a moment. Jehovah's Witnesses love to compare their organization to that of the early nation of Israel who also believed that they were God's chosen people. Jehovah's Witnesses today believe that their organization is similar to that nation of Israel in that there will be a very small number that will be chosen for eternal life by God. The world of global citizens is vastly different today than it was back then. There are about eight million who are professed Jehovah's Witnesses today in a world of about seven billion. The thought here is that almost seven billion people are all wrong and will die at God's hand because they are NOT Jehovah's Witnesses.

Marrying someone who was not specifically a Jehovah's Witness, while not forbidden, was seriously frowned upon. The Witness that married an outsider could expect to find themselves with limited opportunities inside the organization.

I met my soon-to-be wife when I was eighteen, and she was sixteen. She had to be the most beautiful woman from the country I had ever seen in my life. Her parents were East- and West-Indian. She had flawless olive skin, big brown eyes and the healthiest head of hair I had ever seen on a woman. Beauty and grace could have been her middle name. Simply put, I was smitten, taken off my course, relieved of my thinking faculties. She was from a land far, far away. Jehovah's Witnesses hold yearly conventions and assemblies, and those were the only times I could see her. We wrote letters every day and at times, several times a day. Yep, I had fallen in love with this girl. It would be a beautiful engagement, a beautiful wedding, and it would be the marriage to turn my life upside down, taking many years to rightsize.

What happened? I was too damn young! There were not a lot of options for a young man like myself outside of being a Witness. No college hopes or paths to cool secular careers. Being caught up in this organization meant countless meetings, conventions and Saturday morning preaching activities. So, I got married in the hopes of creating my own life and having some sense of control. It really did not work. I wanted so much more for my life. My wife was a hardcore witness, always immersed in the study of religious materials. For a while, I endured successfully. I was many times a featured speaker at some of our yearly conventions. I regularly gave talks at the Kingdom Hall and led the weekend preaching activity. However, I soon became distracted with worldly things. I wanted to go to college, have a career, travel the world, buy things, and have hobbies and interests outside of WATCHTOWER activities. Add to this the financial struggles that came with having no formal education outside of high school fueled my efforts to find something else to add to my life.

She is a good woman. She was a good wife; she was, however, no good for me. We had nothing in common really except these two beautiful boys and the religion we shared. Although it was never really my faith, I accepted it in order to fit in with everyone I had grown up with, my so-called friends. And because we had very little in common with each other, it became very easy for me to find those similar interests in others. By the time I became fed up with trying to live the life of a Jehovah Witness, I was about thirty years old with my first son. After struggling hard to finish a two-year engineering program, I was able to settle into a decent paying career that actually made me feel pretty good about myself and the things I could provide. I bought a nice house in the suburbs, found my sense of style, and started making a few friends and networking with other professional African-Americans in the town I lived, Columbus, Ohio. I had always been a lover of live music. I remember going to this place in German Village, south of downtown Columbus, for a professional networking event. After the initial event had died down, the music started, and I soon noticed that I was surrounded by beautiful black women, something my eyes had been blind to for many years. They were professional, educated women with curvy bodies and great conversations. By my own admission, I was sex starved and hungry for some attention, which I was not getting at home in between all the Bible study, Kingdom Hall meetings, and 'field service' days.

Anyway, I do not remember her name, but I remember her hips—slender, outlined by the dimmed lights and the dark atmosphere of the jazz club. She stood against the wall across the room, her swaying figure holding my eyes waist level only, beckoning me to come dance with her, to touch her hips. Was this woman calling me, wanting me, desiring me? I had never seen anything like this before. The room was crowded, tables everywhere, couples slowly nodding their heads to the rhythmic sounds of horns and drums. Because my eyes were mesmerized by the sexiest hips in the room, my legs would not, could not move, but there I was dancing hip to hip with the beautiful, chocolate brown-eyed goddess and drunk with a newfound sex appeal, I would not hold back.

 My hands found her hips, the small of her back, and a beautiful lump of unholy goodness. My groin was on fire! She was mine for the taking, but I was unprepared for what I felt were uncharted waters. See, I married as a virgin and had never slept with a woman of my own race and felt that I was about to be eaten alive. So, I took her number and excused myself. I went home and spent the next twenty minutes in the bathroom relieving my anxiety. At that moment, I knew I wanted more. I knew I made the wrong choice. I wanted more chocolate in my life, and I needed to unwrap this one and fast!

Before I continue, let me say that I believe firmly in the sanctity of marriage. The family is at the very foundation of society. If we do not maintain the family unit, the world deteriorates. With that being said, it becomes a very different situation when you are in a miserable marriage, and one of the partners refuses to change or to consider any other pathways to marital success. Add to this the importance of compatibility. If two people do not have common interests and goals at the very core of their relationship, things will be different and challenging. Marrying someone on the basis of beauty and brains is not enough. I cannot overemphasize this point. My wife and I did nothing together, despite my constant efforts to do so. I went most places alone. I went to concerts, clubs, the gym, bike rides, walks—almost everything—alone. We were miserable except when we went to the Kingdom Hall. I would smile and invite people over to our home, all the while wanting—begging—to awaken from the nightmare.

Eventually, I mustered up the courage to make a move for a new experience, and so I called the young woman I met at the jazz club. We agreed to meet for lunch later the next day. It was a warm summer day, and she was wearing a gray suit not at all hiding her slender hips and the lump of goodness.

After a long hug, it was impossible for me to cover up my excitement for her body and the experiences I did not know were coming to me in a few hours' time. Incidentally, as I sit here and write this, two young Jehovah Witness men, probably no older than fifteen, just came into Starbucks. I wonder if they have any plans for their future, or will their dreams be derailed by endless calls for their submission to their fears?

Lunch was long and sexy. What was I going to do? I had a new package of condoms in my car. My night was free. I told my wife that I was staying overnight with a project in Southern Ohio, so I had the cover to do what I wanted all night without question. I had prepared myself for this moment, telling myself that my needs were not being met and that God was good in granting me sweet things to eat. So I would eat this chocolate with a clear conscience. God had made it; how could I resist this meal set before me? We ended our lunch, and I went to the gym with the agreement that I would return to her place around eight in the evening. Before I could even reconsider, she gave me the address.

I was an hour late, not because of traffic but because I was sitting outside her condo in my car debating my conscience. Right versus wrong. Need versus want. I decided that I want. I knocked on the door and with nerves of steel took the journey. After sharing a glass of wine and some interesting small talk, the moment took over. Low flames and scented candles only increased the eroticism of the moment. I recall with the clarity of color, the taste of her full lips, and moments later, flesh to flesh the feel of her soft dark skin against mine as I discovered for the first time the insane intensity of being with my first black woman. It was a very, very long night. I loved my wife. I made love to her when the opportunity arose. I did not need any more love in my life. I needed something else.

I needed some fucking! That is what it was. Some of the best fucking in my life! My brain was on fire. Surely, God would destroy me at this moment. As I lay buried between her legs, going deeper and deeper, I thought that I would be paralyzed by God's lightning bolt at any time! However, the deeper I got, the harder I pounded her, and the more she moaned, the more I began to think God was on my side...no lightning bolt. So, I turned her over, and for the first time, I saw the lump of goodness! Harder and LONGER than I had EVER been in my life, I eased into the lump of goodness. For the first time EVER, doggy style had STYLE, and I would never be the same. I rode it hard for all the times I hated being at the Kingdom Hall on game night. I rode it hard for all the times I hated walking door to door, preaching in the snow and heavy cold. I rode the lump or goodness hard for each and every time my snobby wife denied me the same.

I came so hard my brain fell out. It was early morning, and I would never see her again. However, the damage had been done, and soon I would be out on the streets looking for my next fix.

Meanwhile and back at home, my wife was probably wondering where I was, and I really did not care. I was fed up and tired of trying to be the spiritual head of a family everyone wanted me to be. It was not that I did not have a sense of spirituality, I did, and I still do. Living up to the insanely high standards of being one of Jehovah's Witnesses requires that you have this deep, unrelenting love for God, and I just did not have that. I did not feel love for God in my heart at all. I was never overcome with emotions at the very thought of God as is so often illustrated in the Bible, for example, in the book of Psalms. Now there were many days when I was in appreciation for what had been created, the beauty all around me, and, of course, life itself. I spent many days wondering what it might have been like to have lived back in the days of Moses when man had a direct relationship with God without the need of a mediator. At the same time, I was thankful that I did not live in those times for, no doubt, I would be a dead man for making some dreaded misstep. To be honest, I have been scared of God all this time. The very fear of being eaten alive by fire for telling a lie about lusting after some woman in the camp scared me to death!

But is God really that judgmental? Is He really as cruel, mean, and vengeful as I have been taught all these years? Wait, controversy looms. How is God loving, kind, and gentle but at the same time a vindictive bringer of justice upon those 'wicked' people who do not believe or want to worship as he requests? I do not know too many wicked people, but I know they exist, but is the whole world mean? Being raised to believe you are never more than a half step away from being wicked, meriting God's vengeful judgment, is an awful way to live. I always thought I was an evil kid.

For instance, I remember one girl named Katrina. She was a cute young lady that went to my Kingdom Hall. Her family liked me, and I liked them. We all got along well. Her dad thought I might make her a fine husband someday although I was not so sure. I knew she liked me quite a lot, and I was off and on about it. Truthfully if I had stayed with her and married, we would probably still be together today. We had a lot in common. Today, she is married to a fine man, and they have beautiful girls. Anyway, I think Katrina and I started fooling around when I was about seventeen or eighteen. We kissed, held hands, went to the movies, hung out, and did the usual things. However, as you would expect, we eventually started to let our hands do the walking in places we ought not and ended up breaking every single rule in place. I remember one night she came to my job to see me and we ended up getting butt-naked but were careful not to touch genitals for fear of becoming 'wicked' on the spot. We hung out late that night, and I remember the interrogation from my dad the next morning while eating breakfast.

"You stayed out a bit late last night. What did you do?"

My mother was busy cooking more breakfast because old school convention requires that Dad eats first. Therefore, I had nothing else to do but respond to his interrogation.

"I hung out with some of my friends," I replied.

"Who did you hang out with?"

"Some of my friends," unclear as to why I was repeating myself.

My dad ate every meal with a certain seriousness. He kept a crinkled forehead while making hard stabs at the food on his plate as if he had to kill it first.

"Who exactly?" he insisted.

I was eighteen now and was feeling like my privacy was being violated. He was always looking over my shoulders when it came to my friends. Even those at the Kingdom Hall were not good enough it seemed. I wanted to tell him that I was hanging out with my worldly, demon-possessed, drug-addicted, sex-crazed alcoholic friends. I would have wound up with a fork in my eye.

"A couple guys from the Kingdom Hall," I said.

Now, I think he knew better, but if I were to tell him that I was with Katrina and was having a blast fondling her lady parts, I would be buried in the back yard under his vegetable garden.

"Where did you guys go, and who was with you?"

"We went to a party up North, near Westerville, with some friends from the west- and the south-side congregations." It always seemed to me that the congregations on the north, west, and south sides of town had all the fun.

"Well, I hope you were not involved in any loose conduct that might threaten my responsibilities at the Kingdom Hall."

I replied with a blank stare. I certainly was not going to share with him all the "loose conduct" I had been involved in the night before. I was not going to share with him that I was out kissing on a girl from the Kingdom Hall, feeling her womanly parts and getting my grind on. I was just enjoying the simple pleasure of being a teenager and experiencing summer love for the first time. However, this experience would have gotten me disfellowshipped, so I kept my mouth shut.

Chapter 2

So, as a married man, I have now committed the horrible offense of adultery. My conscience is burning, and my brain is aflame trying to figure out how to avoid being disfellowshipped. The idea of being cut off from all of my friends and family was constantly looming in my mind, a fate worse than death itself. However, the process that leads one to being disfellowshipped is actually much worse.

This fear, groomed in you from the beginning of your experience being one of Jehovah's Witnesses can overtake reason and soundness of mind. Could it be that with a stroke of a pen or a verbal announcement to the congregation that you have been disfellowshipped REALLY spell a death sentence? I often wondered if the elders had some sort of verbal contract in place with God himself such that when a person is disfellowshipped, he or she was automatically removed from God's Book of Life. How could an educated and somewhat mature man like me think like this? Fear. Fear and anxiety about a simple judicial meeting had overruled my logical reasoning skills. Where was my soundness of mind? Did I not just cheat on my wife, multiple times? Where was my concern for her? Where was my concern for my family situation? What about the effect this would have on my children? I had just committed acts that would eventually destroy my family unit—which might have been imperfect, but still was my family.

However, with the act of disfellowshipping comes great embarrassment. All of a sudden, people close to you are forced to make excuses for your "bad" conduct, and everything is now judged by a "scriptural" standard often used to bolster the high number of rules as well as the severe penalties paid for even small infractions. People will gossip and talk about you behind your back regarding how they think you came to be judged by God with this draconian punishment. Most, ninety-nine percent, will not have the balls to come to you personally and ask you about your situation, knowing that if they are found out to have spoken to you in your disfellowshipped state, they could experience the same harsh judgment.

I often recall observing the disfellowshipped ones sitting in near isolation, either in the library or the back of the Kingdom Hall off from the rest of the congregation, as if they are quarantined with some awful disease. They often arrive at the meeting late and leave early to avoid having to walk through a large crowd of people conditioned to ignore them, forbidden to speak or even give a warm smile or glance.

So it was the things described above that occupied my mind in the first place where I should have been more worried about my marital situation. As I have gotten older, matured, and moved beyond the pain of my experiences, I am often tortured by how I treated my wife in those years. How I missed the point of being in love, being married, and being responsible for another person. My mind and emotions were clouded with the fear of being deprived of my privileges in the congregations, losing my face in front of others, and being excluded from association with people that I thought were important to my survival. I was gripped by fear, not the fear that comes from disappointing a very close friend, like the fake friendship I had with God, but the fear that comes more from the expectation that this vengeful God would destroy me during the "mystical" Armageddon.

So, when I confessed my adultery to my wife, it was not because I was making some effort at clearing the air in hopes of re-building our relationship based on loyalty and trust. I did it strictly out of fear. Jehovah's Witnesses are taught that no sin can ever be hidden. If you believe like I once did that every sin is seen by God Himself and that He communicates this in some sort of magical way with the elders, you will start thinking about damage control. Imagine being in a police interrogation where you believe the cops have some irrefutable evidence against you, telling you that they may go easier on you if you just admit your guilt—you confess.

I figured that if I confessed to my wife first, then perhaps God would be more forgiving of me when the judgment came. Instead of feeling better about my own misdeeds, I watched as my wife's face filled up with tears. Heartbroken and visibly shaken, she fell to the floor, hitting her head on the corner of the table. I do not recall what happened next or what my reaction was, but I do remember that three days later, I was sitting in a room full of elders.

So here I sit in a place of confession. Where was my wife? Was she suffering? What should I be doing now?

Confession is good for the soul, yet I was riddled with fear, sadness, and uncertainty. What was I doing? Why was I explaining the intimate details of my personal life to these men?

Save yourself. Save your face. Save the shame. Save the questions. Save your marriage?

Elders can come to have knowledge of serious wrongdoing in the congregation two different ways: The wrongdoer confesses, or someone with knowledge of the wrongdoing reports it. In the first case, a judicial committee of three elders is assigned to investigate. However, if the morally wrong act is reported by another, then two elders are appointed to investigate. If the two elders are able to substantiate the act of wrongdoing against the person, then a three-elder judicial committee is formed.

Once this happens, what follows is more like an inquisition than a judicial proceeding. Jehovah's Witnesses will tell you that the purpose of this meeting is to help heal the spiritually sick condition of the person accused of the wrongdoing. But in ninety-nine percent of the cases, the elders who preside over such situations of misconduct are not doctors, psychiatrists or mental health practitioners. The purpose of these judicial meetings with the wrongdoer is to get the person to admit their wrong and then administer counsel by reading some scriptures and trying to move the wrongdoer to some expression of remorse, commonly through an outburst of tears.

The very awareness that a judicial committee is being formed invokes fear. The idea of sitting in front of men that are likely NOT your peers and discussing the details of your sexual sin is mind numbing. The process for those who are not elders in the congregation is not transparent. For years, there has always been a rumor of an 'elders manual' in existence that was used during these procedures to give them step by step instructions, including a profile of what repentance should look like. The elders are told to use it in accompaniment with the scriptures, but I have seen it used many times in lieu of.

Anyhow, the original judicial hearing is always opened with a prayer to God. The idea is that the committee wants to get God's spirit, whatever that is, to be actively involved in the case so that the elders will be Spirit-guided, and the one under inquisition will be compelled to tell the truth with all humility. After the prayer is concluded, you would think that the loving God you have come to respect, love, and adore would be the one in charge of the proceedings and that his loving arms of protection would steer the discussion to safeguard your emotions and to protect your rights. However, nothing is further from the truth. The meetings begin more like a legal discovery; the same way you are questioned by a prosecuting attorney for a felony offense for which you might receive the death penalty.

I would rather face judge and jury for a serious crime than face this religious organization's judicial process. Unlike being in a court of law, you get a little time to prepare, you get no legal representation, you get no discovery from those seeking to prosecute you, and you do not get to call witnesses to speak in your favor or to validate your side of the story. You are left with your own thoughts and your own defense strategy, which is generally flawed because of the cloud of fear that hangs over your faculties. The elders come prepared because they have made an investigation partially or completely by interviewing those who have made the allegations against you.

Anyway, after the prayer is concluded, the chairman of the committee begins by announcing the charges against you. In this particular situation, you are more likely guilty until proven innocent, which makes the proceedings especially difficult because you are immediately put on the defensive. You really have no rights—there is no reading of the defendant's rights before the "trial" begins. Once the charges are announced, there are a series of scriptures that are read to help the defendant realize that the point of this tribunal is to find the truth and assess the errant one's state of repentance. Once this procedure is out of the way, the questioning begins.

Most often, they will start by asking you what happened. I recall this one instance during my committee meeting with the inquisitors where they were trying to figure out my motives for having sex with this woman with whom I had committed adultery. Before I detail the conversation, let me give you a description of each of my tormentors. The first elder was actually fairly likable although I am not sure why or how he got to be an elder. I heard that in his early days, he was quite the womanizer. He was not a bad-looking fellow, although he had this insanely thick-looking mustache over a fairly plump set of lips, soup coolers describe them well. His thin-lipped wife was probably scared of that, or perhaps it reminded her of something else. Anyway, he reminded me of Billy Dee Williams except that he was two feet too short and a bit on the dumpy side. We will call him **I Wanna Be Billy Dee** or **IWBBD** for short.

The second elder was a fairly likable fellow by many, but for me, it was for only one reason. He had this daughter that was just gorgeous beyond words. Whenever she was at the Kingdom Hall, the meetings automatically got less boring. In his defense though, he was smart and gave really interesting sermons from the stage. I always learned something from him. He was very cerebral but a little awkward in social skills. Very fact-oriented. He had this ridiculously thick mustache with no lips. Each time he spoke, all you could do was focus on the mustache. Add to this the fact that he had hips. As a matter of fact, he bore a striking resemblance to W.C. Fields. Have you ever seen a man with hips? We will call him **W.C. Hips.**

The third elder never said much and listening to him was like watching invisible paint dry. His wife was the funny one, however. Every time I saw her at the Kingdom Hall, her hair looked like a bird's nest. He was just a dork, so we will just call him **Dork.** The conversation went something like this:

W.C. Hips: We are here to discuss the charges against you, that being the act of adultery. Do you disagree with these charges?

Me: Yes.

W.C. Hips: What do you think led to you committing adultery?

Me: I wanted to get me some.

W.C. Hips: Get some what?

Me: Blank stare

W.C. Hips: Were you drinking?

Me: No.

W.C. Hips: Were you taking any drugs?

Me: No dude, she was hot, I didn't need drugs or liquor to make me want some.

IWBBD: So, how did this happen?

Me: What do you mean?

IWBBD: How did you end up in this situation?

Me: What situation?

IWBBD: A situation where your morality was compromised.

Me: Oh, having sex?

IWBBD: Yes.

IWBBD: Were you naked?

Me: Why do you ask?

IWBBD: We are getting to your state of mind.

Me: Eventually.

IWBBD: Who got undressed first?

Me: What difference does that make?

W.C. Hips: Did you fondle her?

Me: Yes, yes…oh, God…YES!

Dork: …

I do not know who was getting turned on more by this conversation, them or me. At this point in the interrogation, I decided it was time to leave, as I did not know if they were going to call my penis as a star witness.

Why did I subject myself to all of this? I was really hoping that they were going to offer me some therapeutic insight into my state of mind, but then, they are not therapists. My expectations of being treated with kindness and respect were quickly shattered when the questioning began.

If you have ever visited a therapist, you will know that their very first step is to set you at ease and to make you feel comfortable. Even the surroundings of their office are designed to put the patient at ease, to make them comfortable so that discussing painful events from their past will not be so difficult. They will spend a significant amount of time getting to know your family history, your work, your love life, your personal life, and future ambitions. This may take several meetings to accomplish. Therapists know how important it is to learn about a person's history before they are able to gain some measurable insight into the reasons behind their actions. Therapists are well-educated students of the mind and study behaviors in the very work that they perform, typically holding Masters Degrees and Ph.D.'s

After leaving the therapist, you probably walked away feeling refreshed and rebuilt—do not expect the same from a Jehovah Witness led judicial hearing. The elders are not qualified therapists. The vast majority of them are nothing more than high school graduates, and very few have college degrees in any mental health field. Their main credential, they claim, comes from the Bible itself. Since Jehovah's Witnesses show disdain for most institutes of higher learning, it is highly unlikely that they have the necessary skill set to deal with the complexities of the human mind and the vast variety of human personalities and behaviors that exist in their congregations.

As a younger man, I spent some time with a therapist for some issues I was having related to my experiences with my father. On my very first visit, I was duly impressed by the number of degrees, and the extent of my therapist's education. She seemed uniquely qualified to help me with my problems and made no efforts to judge me for my past actions. There was no reason for me to ask about her qualifications; they were evident on the wall before me and in the way she spoke with me. However, as I sat in the judicial meeting with these three elders, I began to wonder about their qualifications. Beyond their Bible knowledge and their years in the organization, what uniquely qualifies you to deal with the complexities of my mind and accompanying behaviors?

Your first inclination is to go on the defensive, which is totally understandable since, in many cases, the elders make hardly any effort to get to know anything about your mental state or your emotional background to put your actions into context. For them, it is a very black and white issue, and the proceedings are very often rushed. I believe the proceedings are rushed because the body of elders are afraid to have conversations with the erring one of any depth because of their inability to deal with deep emotions and difficult problems that may stem from a person's complicated life history. They try very hard to prove that the misconduct was willful. In reality, they do not understand that many acts of misconduct are intentional but may be based deep in a person's history. If, however, you can summon tears, they feel that you are genuinely moved to regret, and according to the Jehovah's Witness leadership, it serves as a visible sign that a person may be seriously repentant.

Anyone can cry. If you are reading this and have a judicial meeting coming up, grab an onion, rub your fingers with it, and stick them in your eyes. This should bring about a healthy amount of tears, accompanied by some carefully placed sobbing noises along with strategically placed choking sounds. You too will be able to get away with just about anything you want. In all seriousness, when I was a younger man, I once knew a young lady that was involved in some heavy petting activity with another young man and got busted. By 'busted' I mean one of her peers went running to the elders in her congregation and told them what they knew about her conduct. A judicial committee was formed, and she was hauled into a meeting. Heavy petting is a disfellowshipping offense, so I was surprised when she was not disfellowshipped. So when I ran into her some months later, I asked her how in the world she was able to avoid being disfellowshipped, and she told me that lots of tears and heavy sobbing saved her ass.

I loved my kids, loved my wife but hated my marriage. I was supremely bored. My wife and I had nothing in common except the children and the weekly meetings at the Kingdom Hall. After my second son was born, the problems in our marriage started to escalate. I was married to a woman who was simply not going to bend in trying to find common ground with me. Before the act of adultery brought me into a "courtroom" of unqualified, uneducated prosecutors, we had frequently met with the elders to work out our marital problems.

The elders fancy themselves marriage counselors, actually counselors of any sort claiming the Bible and the Organization as their source of expertise. In my particular case, my marriage had problems that they claimed could all be solved by spending more time in family study. Family study is defined as time spent reading the Bible or studying various topics using literature produced by THE WATCHTOWER and

Tract Society which is the corporation behind Jehovah's Witnesses. The Organization has a tendency to simplify an individual's or families' emotional or marital challenges as a problem that can be fixed with extended prayer and deep Bible study, albeit only with their publications. Often, individuals and families come to the elders for help with their complicated problems and are often simply told that their failure to be successful can be blamed on a lack of prayer and deep study. When they fail to see success in this approach, many fall into the sin they were hoping to avoid and may become depressed as a result.

As I mentioned earlier, the proceedings themselves immediately put you on the defensive. You want the elders to understand why you committed the act and that there are probably mitigating circumstances around your situation and that you are not some deviant and wicked sinner hell-bent on corrupting the order and cleanliness of the congregation. In any court of law, you are able to mount a sufficient defense, but not so with the judicial committee. The more time you spend trying to defend your actions, the guiltier you become in their eyes. What this board wants is a straight-up admission of guilt. Admission of guilt without offering any excuses is seen as a show of humility. However, in my particular case, admitting that I committed adultery while married to my wife did nothing to save me from being disfellowshipped.

I had been headed down a wrong road for quite some time during the years I was married and had several meetings with the elders about my course of action. They would always ask me about my study habits, and it was always centered on what was wrong with me. Anytime my wife raised an allegation about my conduct to their attention, conversations were always held with her or me on separate occasions, never together; therefore we never had an opportunity to discuss things openly and honestly with neutral ears. With each meeting I had with the elders, it became very clear to them that I was not interested in following the theocratic order, not interested in complete and total compliance with their rules, regulations, and 'big brother' policies.

I can recall my wife and I having a large number of heated discussions about how we did not really do much of anything together. If I wanted to go to the gym, she did not. If I wanted to go to a club, she did not. If I wanted to do anything outside of going to the Kingdom Hall, or being in the Field Ministry, she was not really interested. Perhaps our problems might have been dealt with more successfully had we visited a marital relations therapist. However, for a Jehovah's Witness to visit a therapist of any kind is to deny the power of the Bible and its influence in your life, so we sought the help of the elders in our local congregation instead.

After multiple visits with congregation elders, I am quite sure they were not surprised when I told them I had committed adultery. Thinking back, I think I said it with an air of arrogance and with a feeling of accomplishment. I remember telling the elders that this was not just a matter of lacking self-control—I could have cheated on her many, many times early in our marriage—it was about something else much deeper. It was about the loneliness I felt in my marriage. It was the lack of affection and attention I got from my wife. It was the lack of compatibilities between us. It was her utter defiance in meeting me half way on anything I wanted to do with my life. It was her unwillingness to accept members of my family for being different from hers. It was the constant pressure I felt to be something or someone that I simply did NOT want to be. It was the weekly acting requirement, being on stage, repeating the script before others, and walking a line so as to fit in with the other WATCHTOWER robots. It was the countless books of rules, policies, and procedures by which every member of the congregation was judged fit or not. It was the fear of enjoying yourself. The fear of being ostracized for doing anything to better yourself or the situation for your family. It was the fear of offending any of the other WATCHTOWER robots. It was the fear of me trying to be me, without judgment.

It was damn near everything. I wanted to be free more than anything else. Free of the tightening and unhappy bond of this marriage. Free from the bondage that was being a Jehovah's Witness. I knew that being disfellowshipped would give me this freedom. Was I prepared for it? How would I view this new found freedom? How would I survive in this harsh and cruel world without my brothers and sisters in the 'truth'?

Freedom is defined as "the power to act, speak, or think as one wants without hindrance or restraint."

Freedom was waiting for me, but I was not ready.

At some point during the inquisition, the Elders decide that it is time to make a decision about your fate, your guilt versus innocence. This usually begins when they ask you to leave the room and await their decision. If you do not exit the room blubbering and sobbing with loud groans and moans, things will probably not go very well for you behind these closed doors. According to popular understanding, the Elders will then pray for God's spirit to direct them to the truth and to help them evaluate the information collected during the inquisition. I remember when I was going through the process. I stood outside with my ear to the door. I do not recall hearing any conversations at all. I really think they may have been back there playing cards or taking naps. Anyhow, after some short period of time, they will call you back into the room and announce your fate. Considering the seriousness of being disfellowshipped, these proceedings actually happen very quickly. In my particular case, it took them about fifteen minutes to make a decision. After I was summoned and their decision was announced to me, they right away began to tell me how I could become reinstated into the congregation. I got up out of my chair and walked out the door without saying a word.

Was I surprised? No, not at all. I knew it was coming. Really, what other choice did they have? I mean these were not doctors or therapists or social workers. They were ill-equipped to deal with my issues, unable to dig any deeper below the surface, limited in understanding of all the years of history and other influences that colored the decisions in my life. I do not recall the elders asking about my tumultuous and often times physically and verbally abusive relationship with my father and how this might have impacted my life to this point as well as my relationship with my wife. I do not recall them asking me about the dark period of my life when I was molested by my father's brother, my uncle. Delving into these issues would bring them into the reality that they are not fit to judge me in any way. During the time I served in the religion, there was this thought that the Bible was perfect and that we were imperfect humans being judged against a perfect standard, the Bible. I was being judged against a perfect standard, by imperfect elders who no doubt had experienced their own moral failings, which, of course, were not up for discussion during my private inquisition. In retrospect, I now feel that they had no right as imperfect men to judge another imperfect person against a seemingly perfect standard as the Bible. Should not that responsibility be held by God who is perfect, who wrote the perfect book for imperfect humans?

How did they know what kind of effect hearing the words "our decision is to disfellowship" would have on me? I recall asking them why they would disfellowship a person out of the seemingly safest place on earth and hand them over to Satan. That did not sound very loving to me. How did they know that I would not go home and commit suicide because I was unable to cope? Did they discuss with me any tried, true, and recognized coping strategies for those who have come before me? Of course not. That would be a very different undertaking, and a human's emotional state cannot be adequately monitored and catered too in a matter of a few hours.

I remember the day as if it was yesterday. After they had made the announcement to me that their decision was to disfellowship, I left right away and went outside to my car. I remember precisely the weather. It was warm and balmy outside. As I drove the fifteen miles or so toward home, there was no radio, no music, and no thoughts. Just stunned silence. What would my parents think? What would I say to my children? After all, it would be publicly announced for all to hear. What would the people in the congregation say about me?

I believe that was the slowest and longest drive of my entire life. Who was I going to talk to about this shameful occurrence? Was there anyone out there who could understand how different this would be? Who could I call? It was at that moment that I realized that there was no one, not a soul. All of my life had been dedicated to living within the imaginary lines of the WATCHTOWER organization.

What was I going to do with myself? How was I going to cope with the silence, the loneliness? Should I take my life? After all, I was disfellowshipped by God himself, right? Since I was doomed to death if Armageddon came tomorrow, why not just save myself the agony and commit suicide and not have to live with the derision that comes with being disfellowshipped? I would revisit this thought many more times in the near future.

All these rapid fire questions in my head, and then I remembered that they called my inquisition a judicial committee. Similar to a court of law, the defendant has rights of appeal. Could I actually appeal my conviction and have my disfellowshipping reversed? What new evidence did I have to support my adulterous ways? Aliens? Mental defect? It did not take me long to decide against that plan.

Typically, once the decision to disfellowship a person is made, you are granted the option to appeal their verdict. This means you will now be forced to meet with six elders, three of which will come from another congregation—always three—that do not know you or the situation. The appeal process is typically a useless affair since they always seem to support each other's decisions. If you waive the appeal process, then the announcement is made to the congregation at the next Kingdom Hall meeting, which in my case was on a Thursday night. You are expected to attend and be present when the announcement is made. The idea is that if you are able to sit through this public whipping, then you are showing a humble spirit. Public humiliation is more like it. I decided not to attend the meeting when my announcement was made. As a matter of fact, I never went back to that specific Kingdom Hall.

Shortly after the announcement of my disfellowshipping, my wife moved out with my two boys. I came home and discovered a brief note along with most of my furniture gone. The first thing I did was to pick up the phone and call my mother. My mother and I have always been very close. My family was gone. I wanted to share with my mother my feelings, my angst. But things had changed. She made it clear to me on the phone that she could not talk to me anymore and then quickly hung up. That was the moment when I realized that life was about to change in some very significant ways. I was now alone to face some of the biggest challenges and changes I would ever see in my life.

CHAPTER 3

So here I am lying in my bed at six in the morning, literally hours after being disfellowshipped, and I have not slept at all during the night. My sleep was tormented by my thoughts. Have you ever been awakened in the middle of the night, and you just knew something bad was about to happen, and yet you knew there was nothing you could do to stop it? You might compare it to an inmate that has just been sentenced to be executed unjustly, knowing he is either innocent of the crimes or more likely unfairly or harshly punished.

For the past several years, I owned a technology company that provided services to the prison system in my state of residence. I saw firsthand how inmates on death row were kept under strict control and surveillance, locked down twenty-three hours out of the day with very limited communication and closely monitored at that. It may sound a bit dramatic to compare being disfellowshipped to being condemned to death row. But really, the circumstances are quite similar. When you are disfellowshipped from the organization, it is as though you are dead in their eyes and in the eyes of God, with no real hope for the future until or if you ever get reinstated. Being in the business I was, I was able to learn of several inmates that had committed suicide out of sheer depression and frustration.

Similar to being in prison and on death row, your movements and associations are closely monitored and controlled. Infractions can lead to further punishment. You have no decision-making authority as to when you can recreate, eat or for that matter, even get out of prison. Once you are disfellowshipped, you have no rights. You have no power. You have no say. You are even very limited legally. Some have even tried suing the WATCHTOWER organization with no success because the laws recognize that a religion has the right to operate for the most part as they see fit.

I felt utterly helpless. I had been banned to a prison-like existence with no visiting schedule from friends or family. Banned to a spiritual wilderness with the nagging thought that neither God nor any of the people I cared for felt concern for me anymore.

Committing adultery had gotten me disfellowshipped, thrown out of the congregation, and segregated from my family, children, and friends. But the crazy part of this whole story is that you can get disfellowshipped for FAR less. Yes, you can have your life destroyed for simply smoking or telling a lie. While I am not suggesting that lies and smoking are okay, it does seem like such an offense should not merit having your whole life and family destroyed because of it.

Jehovah's Witnesses consider many actions to be "serious sins" for which a person may be disfellowshipped or shunned. The idea is to remove people from the congregation who might influence other members toward a wayward lifestyle.

Disfellowshipping is a form of discipline that includes forbidding a person from having any contact or association with any other member of the congregation. This will include believing family members such as children, parents, all relatives, and friends. The congregation members are prohibited from speaking to or having any association with one who is being shunned. Disfellowshipped persons are required to attend Kingdom Hall meetings on a weekly basis if they have any hopes of being reinstated, often times for months and years, all while being shunned.

While it is true that most religions have in place some number of policies and rules that must be abided by and some consequences for living outside of those rules, the punitive measure of disfellowshipping is quite extreme even for fringe Christianity.

Interestingly, the word "Disfellowship," or any derivative of it, is not found in the Bible. Jehovah's Witnesses have a long list of offenses for which you can be disfellowshipped:

- Adultery
- Abandoning wife and eloping with another woman
- Planned adultery to break Scriptural marriage ties
- Remarriage without Scriptural permission
- Polygamy
- Dating a person not legally divorced
- Apostasy
- Rebellion against Jehovah's organization
- Promoting sects and cults

- Associating with disfellowshipped people including friends and family
- Blood and blood transfusions
- Drug use
- Drunkenness
- Dishonest business practices
- Employment violating Christian principles
- Working for any religious organization
- Working in a gambling institution
- Selling tobacco
- Contract work at a military establishment
- Attending another church
- Following mourning customs that involve false worship
- Fornication
- Bestiality
- Incestuous marriage
- Artificial insemination
- Sexual abuse of children
- Fraud
- Gambling or related employment
- Gluttony

- Greed
- Gambling
- Extortion
- Homosexuality
- Idolatry
- Loose conduct
- Disregard for Jehovah's moral standards
- Disrespect, disregard or even contempt for standards, laws, and authority,
- Lying
- Military service and non-military service
- Obscene speech
- Political involvement, including voting or holding a political office.
- Porneia. "It includes oral and anal sex or mutual masturbation between persons not married to each other, homosexuality, lesbianism, fornication, adultery, incest, and bestiality."
- Slander
- Smoking or selling tobacco
- Spiritism, including yoga
- Stealing, thievery

- Subversive activity
- Uncleanness
- Sexually "perverse" practices within marriage, such as oral and anal sex
- Heavy petting and breast fondling
- Touching of sexual parts
- Violation of secular law if flagrant attitude
- Violence, extreme physical abuse, fits of anger
- Boxing
- Willful nonsupport of family, endangerment of mate's spirituality
- Worldly celebrations such as Christmas

After putting together this list, you must be thinking the same as me: Good grief, what a list! You could wake up in the morning on the wrong side of your thoughts and be disfellowshipped by noon. All kidding aside, how do you enjoy a guilt-free conscience before God and others when your very thoughts will condemn you, never mind your actions? It has long been taught by the Jehovah's Witnesses that a person who is disfellowshipped is not only seen as unfit in the eyes of fellow witnesses but is also considered dead in the eyes of their God, Jehovah, and therefore, unworthy of all the glorious promises of life, along with the resurrection that they say await those who remain in good standing. So, you can imagine that for most witnesses, the act of being disfellowshipped escalates the mind-numbing fear of everlasting death and destruction.

Simple internet searches will yield thousands of results around people who have been disfellowshipped and the horrible feelings of isolation and desperation they felt. There are many stories of depression, suicide attempts, and the total destruction of once strong family relationships. Children's lives have been destroyed, marriages ruined, and many healthy minds mangled.

Before we continue, a little history about this religion would do the reader good here. Many of the current members have no idea where their religion originated or even the background of the founders and early leaders, although an extraordinary amount of solid research is available on many websites. A list of resources for independent research about Jehovah's Witnesses can be found on the resources page at the end of this book. Let me give you a bird's eye view.

Jehovah's Witnesses, originally known as the International Bible Students, first came into existence as an organization in 1879 under the leadership of Pastor Charles Taze Russell. The foundation of his message was that based on various biblical chronology and certain events being played out on the global stage, the world would be ending very soon and that there would be a very small number of persons that would survive this cataclysmic event called Armageddon. An event of global destruction began and ended by God himself meant to cleanse the world of all its evil. Only those people who had attached themselves to Pastor Russell's organization would survive.

Jehovah's Witnesses have a long history of vocally predicting the end of the world with zero survivors except themselves. The more recent and famous dates for world destruction have included 1914, 1925, and most recently, 1975. In each of these predictions, it was understood by Jehovah's Witnesses that billions would be killed by God with those surviving numbering into nothing more than the few million Witnesses around the globe. Jehovah's Witnesses are also well known for their religious practices seen by many to be outside the margins of Christianity. These include the refusal of blood transfusions, the prohibition on celebrating holidays such as Christmas, Halloween, Easter, Birthdays, and any other holiday except for the Memorial of Christ Death as they call it.

In more recent history, Jehovah's Witnesses have been plagued by accusations of child abuse and of harboring pedophiles in their local congregations through policies of secrecy that the leadership refuses to acknowledge or adjust. The recent success of several highly publicized child abuse cases and subsequent judgments will likely lead to an onslaught of lawsuits against the organization.

As of this writing, Jehovah's Witnesses boast a worldwide membership of nearly eight million members.

I recall that when I was young in the organization and people asked me about my religious beliefs, I would promptly and proudly tell them that I was one of Jehovah's Witnesses. Generally, their first response was to say that we were a cult. Our programmed response was to insist that we were not a cult because we did not follow any one man. This generally shut the conversation down because most had in memory recent tragic events where a cult members' following of the lunacy of one person resulted in the deaths of hundreds and sometimes even thousands.

In fact, you might call Jehovah's Witnesses a "super cult" because they follow not one man, but seven, known as the governing body.

This reasoning served well to keep the rank and file from asking deeper questions, and I seriously doubt any of us took the time to try and understand what is intimated by the word "cult."

Almost any type of institution can be defined as a cult. We go to work and follow certain rules and are rewarded when we follow them with a paycheck.

We go to school and follow the norms of the administration, and when we are successful, we earn diplomas. Some cults can be dangerous if they use their sphere of influence to deliberately inflict harm on others. History is full of extremist organizations that use the loyalty of their followers to further their agenda through the use of violence. Not all cults are violent. Not all cults are dangerous.

Jehovah's Witnesses are a dangerous *and* destructive cult.

In his book, *Combating Cult Mind Control*, Steven Hassan defines a destructive cult as any "group that's engaged in outright deception to pursue its ends, whether those be religious, economic or political" (1). Through standard indoctrination, Jehovah's Witnesses are slowly mind-controlled to the point where they are encouraged to give up their hopes, dreams, their long time association with friends and family, replacing them with their new "family" at the Kingdom Hall. Now, I know you must think I am being a bit dramatic because I used the term "mind control." To many, that might conjure up a science fiction movie and a science lab with lots of whizzing electronics manned by a mad scientist. Mind control is a science. My favorite cult expert, Hassan, explains: "mind control may be understood as a *system* of influences that disrupts an individual's identity (beliefs, behavior, thinking, and emotions) and replaces it with a new identity" (2).

Identity, the state of being who or what you are. This is an important concept to consider. Knowing who you are is part of the driving force that gets you up each day, the force that causes you do the things that you do. Your identity is something that is developed organically, naturally within you over time. Your identity can be the result of many inputs in life, your passions, your pursuits, your knowledge, your desires, your needs, and the list goes on. A forced identity is not a natural one. Being indoctrinated by a cult is an identity imposed by coercion. It goes against your natural inclinations of who you think you should be, who you want to be. Forced identity is like being in prison—an analogy I use often. When you go to jail, who you were on the outside does not matter anymore. You are a captive of the state, a prisoner with a number and a daily routine over which you have no control. However, for some prisoners, the expiration of a sentence means freedom awaits them along with the need to realize their true identity. Without taking the time to do this, these individuals often end up right back in their prison.

Identity imposed by coercion is called a pseudo-identity. It is not the real you.

From my earliest memories as a child, my indoctrination began. For many others, their indoctrination may have started in their early adulthood. It is very likely that they had a sense of themselves before coming into contact with the cult and so upon leaving may find it a bit easier to return to some resemblance of whom they were prior. This may prove easier for them as they may have family members and friends that are not part of the cult and will help them to reorient themselves in normal society.

For others, like me, this is not so easy. Perhaps most, if not all of your friends, are fully mind-controlled.

A cult by its very nature is likely to violate our human rights. We have thirty fundamental human rights, and most of us take our abilities to exercise them for granted. However, those being mind-controlled by cultish religions like Jehovah's Witnesses will not even recognize their lack, much less be able to take the necessary steps to rightsize.

During my time as one of Jehovah's Witnesses, I would suggest that at least eight of my basic human rights were being trampled on a daily basis just by being affiliated with this group. Consider:

Free and Equal. No one is equal. There are elders, ministerial servants, pioneers, special pioneers, circuit overseers, district overseers, lowly publishers, and a hoard of other titles given as rewards of performance to set them apart from others. If you do not hold a title, then you can be seen as being less approved by Jehovah. This, of course, affects your social standing in the congregation. No one wants to associate with just a "publisher."

Do Not Discriminate. Jehovah's Witnesses are elitists. All others do not really matter much. They have no tolerance for anything that does not walk, talk, smell, dress or act like them. They discriminate against all outsiders until or unless you become one of them. Once you are one of them, the discrimination is based on your congregation position, how many hours you spend preaching, how active you are in organizational activities or how fat your pockets are. Jehovah's Witnesses love to work in the trades. If you suffer a natural catastrophe, they will come in and rebuild their Kingdom Halls, but unless you can profess your allegiance to the WATCHTOWER Bible & Tract Society, do not expect much help from them.

The Right to Life. Everyone knows that Jehovah's Witnesses take exception to blood transfusions as a part of their doctrine. For an organization that preaches about the value of life, they let hundreds if not thousands of their members die by insisting that taking blood transfusions to save a person's life is against God's Biblical law.

The Freedom of Thought. Questioning or expressing any dissatisfaction with doctrines or procedures can get you disfellowshipped, shunned, kicked out of the organization. Controlling what and how members think is the key to keeping them penned in. For many years, surfing the internet was forbidden, advising parents to keep computers in open spaces so these could be monitored. Reading literature not provided by the Society is prohibited and is constantly referred to as "apostate material." If members are afraid to discuss their concerns with each other, then dissenting thoughts and logical arguments for and against are never considered.

The Freedom of Speech. What is that?

The Right to Education. The Organization provides you with all the education you need, especially since Armageddon, the end of the world, is "right around the corner." Why would you let the "empty philosophies of men" keep you from surviving the end of the world? What worth can a college education bring you? Surely a college education will make it impossible for you to worship God and earn a living, right? As a result of this thinking, millions of Jehovah's Witnesses live less than the great lives they could be living. Many are living paycheck to paycheck, unqualified for many of the best jobs, accepting that their future will not be in retirement but in menial jobs until they die. They are under constant pressure to give a portion of their meager earnings to fill the coffers of the publishing company and property developers they worship. If you ever find yourself in need of a housekeeper or a janitor for your business, just stop by your local Kingdom Hall and get a few quotes.

The Right to Privacy. One might suppose that within the family circle there can be an expectation of privacy. Not so much if you are part of a Jehovah's Witness family. Do not take privacy for granted if you whisper dissenting thoughts on doctrine to your spouse; they just might tell on you. Or if, as a married couple, you were hoping for a hot night of steamy oral sex, you would need to be careful as your marriage partner may report that to the elders. Can you imagine some old man asking you if your wife is giving you blow jobs? Under the disguise of "keeping the congregation clean" members are encouraged to report anything and everything that might bring reproach on Jehovah or challenge the cleanliness of the congregation. How does making your spouse have an orgasm with parts of your face give a bad reflection on God? He made this stuff, didn't He?

The Right to A Fair Trial. Approach any baptized Jehovah's Witness and announce that a judicial committee has been formed to investigate their conduct, and you would have just doomed this person to a week of sleepless nights, diarrhea, and perhaps a date with a shotgun. You get little time to prepare a defense, you cannot cross-examine the witnesses against you, questioning the judicial committee members is not allowed, you are guilty from the beginning, and appealed decisions are rarely reversed. There is nothing fair about that.

So here I was. Disfellowshipped, and despite the reasons, the action was taken.

I should have been thankful, should have had the vision to see that I had been set free from the harshness and enslavement of belonging to this organization. To the contrary, my mind turned immediately to my loss; the loss of my friends, family, and my sense of self.

So, what was I going to do? I certainly was not going back to the Kingdom Hall. The elders encourage those that have been disfellowshipped to sit in the back rows of the hall as if that were a visible sign of punishment. After having my name read off the stage as being 'disfellowshipped', there was no way in the world I was going to be further humiliated by being told where I could sit in a public place. It would be many months before I would ever attend another meeting. I did not know how I would respond to people who at one time were my friends, my "brothers and sisters," ignoring me and not speaking to me. As of matter of fact, I really had no idea how far many would go to meet the requirements for how to treat disfellowshipped people.

Since I was adamant that I was not going back to a Kingdom Hall or any other Jehovah's Witness event, I now had a lot of extra time on my hands. There was no one in my circle anymore except for my work colleagues. But since as a devout Jehovah's Witness, I was taught to hold those not in our religion in derision and consider them not worthy of my time or consideration; I was more alone in the world than the average person. I had not taken the time to get to know my workmates, their families or their interests. I was scared of them. I was taught to be fearful of their external thoughts, to be wary of them so as to avoid having my pure spiritual standing tainted. My learned elitist attitude toward others, while tolerated in the Kingdom Hall as normal and expected, would make it tough for me to find a place and to make a few good friends outside of the cultish organization. During my years as an active witness, there really was no time to be lonely or to worry about making new friends. There were meetings at the Kingdom Hall twice during the weekdays and at least twice on the weekends, not including the extra time you might spend in the ministry knocking on doors, looking for more mindless, non-thinking minions to join the ranks. There were always people around you. There was always some level of association or interaction.

But now I did not have that. I did not have a place to go on Tuesday and Thursday evenings. My Saturday mornings were free as well as my Sundays. When the decision was made to disfellowship me by the Jehovah's Witness clowns, I recall them telling me not to associate with 'worldly' people—that is the official classification of Jehovah's Witness non-believers. I was encouraged not to go to clubs, not to associate with other disfellowshipped persons, not to talk to those in good standing at the Kingdom Hall, stay away from churches, and more importantly, not to read articles or visit websites authored by ex-Jehovah's Witnesses. For me, such dire warnings to stay away from the Internet and their "apostate" websites would eventually be instrumental in helping me gain my freedom.

Since I had not decided that this was not my truth anymore, I had desires of returning, although not for the right reasons. I did not have any clear idea as to how I was going to survive without this organization, my parents, and my pseudo-friends in the congregation. My fears of being destroyed at Armageddon and not making it into the paradise were simply paralyzing. Everything I thought about was governed by this fear of exclusion. But the reality was that I was not a part of this organization anymore. I was so indoctrinated I truly believed that no other religious group out of the seven billion people on the earth could ever have God's approval but the Jehovah's Witnesses, so there was no way I was going to stretch out and explore any other ideas, let alone visit a church.

I could not think. I could not strategize. I could not develop a roadmap to move forward. I was simply trapped in a cycle of extreme control, like a rat who wants to do nothing more than to get back into the cage, on the wheel, and eat the same old dry cheese and bread, even though he was set free from his imprisonment.

For a long while, still intent on getting reinstated and with some twisted hope that I would be readmitted to the Jehovah's Witness organization, I spent most of my nights and weekends at home out of fear that somehow the elders would come to know my every movement and that I might be associating with worldly people or surfing the internet, which would keep me from being reinstated into the congregation. I would never in life have ever considered myself to be a sad person or even depressed. However, at this point, I would soon be suffering the typical symptoms of depression. I rarely left the house. I had no visitors. I rarely saw my boys, never cleaned the house, or myself for that matter, and rarely ate any kind of healthy food. Exercise was out of the question. The gardening work and lawn care that I once loved to engage in was a thing of the past. Everything I loved to do with my time was uninteresting at this point.

I was depressed. I was incredibly alone. My parents would not even return my call, even when they had not heard from me in six months after being disfellowshipped, even when my cell phone was turned off because I did not care to pay the bill. Not once did my parents knock on my door or make any inquiries to see how I was doing. I went through periods of depression so severe that I often thought about committing suicide. I would never consider taking my life in such a deliberate way by using a gun, but I took substantial liberties with my life by driving at high speeds after drinking heavily in the early morning hours. There were countless times when I woke up in my bed not sure how I got there but seeing my car parked in the yard, on the grass, was a clue that the night before was a wild one.

As related earlier, Jehovah's Witnesses strongly discourage the use of psychiatrists and psychologists, opting to use the Bible as their only authority. I could have used their expertise because my destructive behavior was only just getting started. I had no idea who I was. My whole identity had been defined by this organization. Once you leave, either willingly or through expulsion, there is very little social support to help you get back on your feet or to find yourself.

 I needed to make some friends, and since I was newly single, I decided I would start hanging out and was soon swallowed up in my constant search for acceptance and validation. Since I had been expelled from the organization, my feelings of self-worth had been decimated. No longer was there a place for me to go where people knew me, and greetings were exchanged with small talk about our week, the family, the children, and upcoming events.

The loneliness was unbearable. I would go to extreme lengths to create the illusion that I was still a part of this ridiculous organization as I just did not know how to break free from their hold. Even at this stage in my life, there are still minute traces of their influence in my everyday living, in the choices I make or in the fears that manifest from time to time. At one particular time, I was living in Atlanta, and I knew from day to day the schedule of the Witnesses in the local congregation where I attended. I knew where they stopped for breaks in the morning during their door-to-door ministry. I knew where they went to lunch on Saturday and Sundays, where to see them during the week, even some of their grocery habits. All of this in an effort to get someone to acknowledge me, to see me and give me some sign that I was still their friend and that I still had some value in their eyes.

Nothing. It was as if I was invisible. They would look through me as if I was not there, as if looking at me would cause their eyes to be stricken from their sockets. By the way, 'stricken' is a word often used in the Bible and more often by the WATCHTOWER as a word that simply invokes fear. It is this fear that keeps Jehovah's Witnesses from acting with human compassion toward others in their course of blind, unquestioning obedience to what is often referred to as the 'Organization'.

Once I was walking in the mall minding my own business, having a pretty good day, here comes a whole family from the local congregation. As I approached them, I noticed that they were laughing and having a great time amongst themselves. As I got closer to them, and as if they obeyed some unseen commander, they lowered their faces and their voices as they marched on past me. I was stunned by their reaction to me. Did I look ugly that day? Had I forgotten to groom myself according to proper WATCHTOWER standards? As they walked past, I turned around and stared them down as they turned to eye the abomination that dared to walk on the same ground as them. I felt like an outcast in junior high school.

I was no longer permitted inside of this organization which had high control over its members. Yet as an outsider, how did they still have so much power over my life? Why was my every waking moment spent trying to figure out how to get back inside of something that I only wanted to rebel against?

CHAPTER 4

It is a matter of social control. Social control generally applies to societal and political mechanisms or processes that regulate individual and group behavior in an attempt to gain conformity and compliance to the rules of a given society or social group. This definition can very well apply to religious sects and has found practice inside the organization of Jehovah's Witnesses. Once you have met their high standards for admission to their social landscape and with the ongoing requirements to remain, leaving successfully is very difficult.

Most people view the word 'control' as a negative and would not willingly submit to having their lives come under the jurisdiction of any person or organization. It is equally difficult to imagine that

Jehovah's Witnesses willfully set out to create or even execute a method of control. The organization disguises their methods of social control by misusing and misapplying the scriptures to inculcate a feeling of superiority amongst their members while administering a program of exclusion.

The organization creates the illusion that anyone that does not believe as they do is a 'worldly person' not fit for a regular association. They create the fear that these worldly people might influence their members toward a wayward way of life so as to lose their relationship with God and miss out on everlasting life in the so-called paradise. This illusion is so great that it permeates their ministry, their speech, and their actions toward outsiders. While other religious organizations are helping others in need by providing food, clothing, and shelter, Jehovah's Witnesses view those outsiders as unworthy of such material assistance until they become part of their social circle. They teach that Jehovah will fix everything for all people in the promised New World and that there is limited value in material assistance instead offering Bible studies, books, and magazines to satisfy the need today.

Members of the sect are taught to hate the 'things of the world'. This includes all the so-called 'trappings' and pursuits of the 'worldly people', the non-believers. For example, the pursuit of higher education is strongly discouraged. Their illicit reasoning is that they need to cherish and protect the Christian mind from the infiltration of worldly ideas. They generously refer to higher education as "the philosophies of men." They focus on the idea that higher education will introduce their minds to theories and ideals that will wreck their pure understanding of truth and overexpose them to demonic teachings. They do not want to encourage critical thinking because it may lead to questions and, as can be expected, some level of dissent. Only the organization has final say on every matter because, according to them, they have God's spirit.

By disparaging knowledge, apart from that dispensed by the so-called 'Faithful and Discreet Slave', and discouraging biblical research outside of their publications, they effectively keep everyone on the same level playing field. Everyone talks the same talk and walks the same path as the other, at least in public. Exorbitant pressure is exerted upon those inside to not question doctrine, decisions made by the elders or the organization and to wholeheartedly accept all doctrinal changes, no matter how outrageous. To think, to question, to proffer any alternative ideas, beliefs, translations, considerations, explanations or challenges to current doctrine is enough to get you disfellowshipped or shunned from the social circle, equivalent to something like a social death. This means that you will be cut off, as if dead, from all of your friends and family that are currently in "good standing" with the organization. You will not be able to speak or be spoken to. Your very existence will cease. You will not be recognized any longer at any Jehovah's Witness meetings, assemblies or conventions. If you take the opportunity to speak to another Jehovah's Witness while in a disfellowshipped state and are seen by another Jehovah's Witness, that individual will be warned, and if he continues to have conversations with you, he risks being disfellowshipped himself.

Once in my disfellowshipped state and while attending one of our yearly conventions, I was inadvertently drawn into a conversation during the noon break.

Someone who knew of my status approached and announced that I was 'disfellowshipped'. All at once, the small group gave me a look of disdain and quickly scurried away. While I was embarrassed for myself, I was more so at how gripped they were at the fear of being seen having a conversation with another human being. After all, did being disfellowshipped make me any less human? In fact, it made me more human as it showed that I am not perfect and that mistakes are in our very DNA. The ultimate goal for all Jehovah's Witnesses is to obtain perfection, and they spend their lives trying to earn this as their salvation.

In 2012, I attended a District Convention for the sole purpose of seeing my youngest son participate in a dramatization. He had a large part to play with many speaking lines. Even though I no longer agree nor participate in any Jehovah's Witness activities, I thought it was very important to show my support for the things that he places value in. After his part and during the intermission, he and I were having a private conversation about his performance. During that time, my parents and a host of adults I have known since childhood approached and took over the conversation without acknowledging, speaking or even looking my way. This is somewhat to be expected. It is noteworthy to mention that I was freely visiting and having conversation with my parents just several days before this took place. According to Jehovah's Witness policy, they were to have absolutely nothing to do with me. Their snub at the convention was a direct result of social pressure. Hypocrisy at its finest.

For many, the social construct becomes more important than the beliefs themselves. The risk of losing access to the social construct is so strong that many members will suppress their doubts and concerns over the sect's rich history of changing doctrines, shifting views and politics.

So how does this happen? Does the cult have a process for recruiting and onboarding people to be a part of the social construct? Actually, they do. There are a number of social control theories put forth by prominent sociologists that find parts of their ideals used in religion, and Jehovah's Witnesses are not the only ones to practice some measure of social control to maintain their authoritarian hold. I cannot say that the Jehovah's Witnesses' leadership has intentionally implemented the ideals of popular social control theorists like Travis Hirschi, but there are some similarities.

So, what makes Jehovah's Witnesses so successful and why do they continue to thrive? No one wakes up in the morning and decides that they want to be mind-controlled by a cult. We all have a need to belong to something, to have a place to socialize and be amongst people that share things in common with us. Isolation is against our human nature, everyone needs love, friendship, attention and approval in our lives. There is no doubt that the WATCHTOWER Bible and Tract Society (WTBS) is well aware of this human nature. This, in itself, is not enough to ensnare a person; there needs to be a component of lack, the sense that something is missing in their lives, a great sense of loss works even better.

It all begins with a knock at the door and a healthy dose of fear.

Having grown up in the sect, I recall many times when we were being assigned our door-knocking territories that if we ever hoped to speak to anyone and garner some interest, we needed to be working the poorer neighborhoods. Reason being, they were the ones that would be more likely to respond to our message. It is very important to craft a gloom and doom message around some bit of recent bad news. "Did you hear about the recent earthquake in Japan or the recent murder spree in your city? How about the recent rash of deadly diseases in the Congo? What about the recent economic crash? Can you imagine a time in the future when such disasters would be a thing of the past? Under God's Kingdom arrangement such devastating events would come to an end." This is usually followed by a request to read a supporting scripture. Further conversation would outlay the possibility that life is very uncertain and that we need to look forward to a time in the future when God's Kingdom will wipe away all such fears, crime, and early death, with a promise of life on a peaceful paradise earth, with no wicked people or natural disasters to interrupt their peace.

Jehovah's Witnesses at the time when I was heavily involved were required to attend five instructional meetings during the week. One of those was the Theocratic Ministry School or TMS. During the TMS, we were taught tactics to help us get the interest of the 'householder' (a patented term only to be used by Jehovah's Witnesses under threat of certain death). For example, before knocking on a householder door, we are encouraged to take a moment and look for a way to find some common ground for discussion. Perhaps we see toys in the front yard indicating that small children may be in the house. You might approach the householder with the following: "Good morning, my name is so and so, and I noticed that you have small children in the home. Are you concerned about their future, their safety in school and other settings?" They then proceed to expound on the fear parents already have of their children suffering violence at the hands of another. Usually, at about this time, they might present a WATCHTOWER or AWAKE! Magazine or some other brochure that underscores the topic. The answer is to save yourselves and your children from this fate by studying with the Witnesses and getting a ticket to the 'paradise'.

Always looking to capitalize on the householder's bad news, the ideal situation is if the householder has experienced a death in the family. The first play is one of sympathy followed by empathy. The Jehovah's Witnesses may then choose to inquire of their belief by asking this question: "So what is your hope to see your loved one again?" Answers here will vary, but most will answer that they hope to see them in heaven. The Witness here has a choice based on their replies, but most will offer to read a scripture that raises the hope that they might see them again during a resurrection of the dead on a paradise earth where they will have the chance to live forever and ever in perfect health.

This generally sounds really good to the person holding the door open, and if the message has been effective, a Bible study will be offered. Once the Bible study starts, so does the mind job. The Witness then becomes the Bible study conductor. Ideally, they will like to conduct the Bible study at least once per week and at least one-hour long. The student is expected to study the material vigorously before the weekly visit by the Witness Bible study conductor. At first, the Bible studies are conducted very informally, but in short order, the Bible study conductor will show the importance of opening and closing each study with a prayer to Jehovah.

The idea here is that they want to convince the student that their new found knowledge would not and could not be possible without God's blessing. This generally happens within the first few weeks of the Bible study program. Shortly after this, the Scripture study conductor will start to bring other Witnesses to the study. They will generally be prepped with some great new truth to share or will have some incredible insight to offer the new Bible student. For instance, suppose that during the weekly Scripture studies, the conductor realizes that the student has a serious addiction to cigarettes. The Bible student may well know that smoking cigarettes is a habit not tolerated by Jehovah's Witnesses. The Bible study conductor may bring a brother or sister from their local Kingdom Hall who has overcome cigarette smoking successfully before becoming one of Jehovah's Witnesses. This person will tell their story and say that they could not have overcome their habit had it not been for the help they received from Jehovah and his 'spirit-directed' organization. Bringing along someone who also had a problem with cigarettes helps create "common ground" on which to teach but also serves another purpose:

To get them to the Kingdom Hall.

Each week during the Ministry School, a program designed to teach congregation members on the secrets of recruiting converts, they are constantly reminded that to fully indoctrinate their Bible students, they need to get them to the Kingdom Hall. Of course, such words like 'indoctrinate' will never be used in these meetings, but this is the most appropriate word. Getting the new Bible student to the Kingdom Hall is critical as it introduces them to this incredible group of loving and ridiculously caring people. Now, just to be honest, many Jehovah's Witnesses are some of the humblest and nicest people you will ever meet, however, severely misguided and gullible.

The first time a Bible student attends the Kingdom Hall, he is usually given a tour and is introduced to the friendliest of Witnesses in attendance. The warmth is generally overwhelming, and the Bible student feels like they have walked into something of a paradise. During subsequent Bible studies, the student is encouraged to view these new associates as their "brothers and sisters, mothers and fathers in a spiritual sense." The new member is also advised that all others that are not worshipping the one true God are outside of His favor and are a risk to maintaining a healthy relationship with their Creator. After all, you have been shown the 'truth', why would you want to jeopardize your chances at eternal life on a paradise earth by associating with those who are outside of God's favor?

The push continues for the prospective recruits to attend as many meetings at the Kingdom Hall as possible to socialize them into the brotherhood. The more the new recruit attends the Kingdom Hall and socializes with their new 'brothers and sisters', the more he feels his current social circle is not worthy anymore. This new social group exerts pressure on the new person as they make "spiritual progress" to cut (or severely reduce) ties with those in their families and social circles who may not fully support their new belief systems.

After some arbitrary amount of time and Bible studies and after approval by the elders in the congregation where the new recruit and their instructor attend, he may be permitted to participate in the preaching work. If the student wants to become one of them and live in their "spiritual paradise" and have a "shot" at everlasting life on the paradise earth, he must learn to actively participate in the door-to-door ministry. No support is given for the painfully shy or any other social disease the new student may suffer from that cannot be overcome by God's spirit. Participating regularly in the door-to-door ministry is a requirement before you can graduate to the next step: being approved for baptism. There is much more that can be discussed here on the subject of participating in the ministry. There are some who genuinely want to march door to door with a message in hand, confident that their variety of good news is surely what is needed as we stand behind our doors waiting for that fateful knock or doorbell ring. But for the majority, participation is a matter of social pressure.

I cannot tell you how many times I have sat in the Kingdom Hall and countless conventions to hear these incredible stories of how someone was having thoughts of suicide on the day that the Witnesses knocked on their door and interrupted either the act or the thought. I have spent an unimaginable amount of time knocking on doors over my lifetime, and I have yet to come upon a single person that has admitted that they were about to commit suicide or that I interrupted their gun lunch. Typically, you will start hearing of these experiences when field service reporting on hours begins to dip, or a trend is noted that shows a lack of participation in the preaching activity.

This typically works. Most of my experiences have resulted in either getting a door slammed in my face or being told just to go away, often not in a very polite fashion. However, if you are sitting in the audience hearing experiences that other witnesses are having, like the one mentioned above, you will feel excited and motivated to spend more time and recommit to your evangelizing. Perhaps God will bless you with such an experience of saving a life with your message.

So, imagine if you are a student studying with Jehovah's Witnesses, and you hear how they are engaged in this preaching activity and saving people from committing suicides, you will surely wonder how this is possible or how they know. You will be told over and over that God is using angels to direct this work. They will show you wonderfully illustrated magazines and brochures that picture God's angelic creatures invisibly directing Saturday morning porch thumpers to that person who is in desperate need of your message. When this idea is repeatedly presented, it becomes very powerful, and you begin to believe without adequate and reasonable support that Jehovah's Witnesses are the only ones involved in a lifesaving work that is directed by holy spirit and angels. How could you not want to spend your weekends and evenings walking door to door with these messages of hope?

So the new student puts on a tie or a dress and hushes their pangs of anxiety and begins to learn the messaging and the methodology for trotting the streets looking for new recruits. Once the Bible teacher and the elder body are satisfied that the student has put away all of their evil ways and has committed to a life of door knockin', street walkin', and book hawkin', that student may then apply to be baptized into the new social order. This is a very formal process where the student must sit in front of two elders and answer to their satisfaction a number of questions designed to ascertain their Bible knowledge and their spiritual fitness. If they successfully pass this test, and most will, then they are authorized to be baptized in water as a formal indication that they have walked away from their former way of life, including their worldy friends and family, no matter how important.

You are one of us now. We are your family. You cannot leave. We have you.

CHAPTER 5

Baptism is the final frontier. If there were ever a last chance to bolt for the door with ZERO consequences, this would be the time. Do you have doubts? Run! Do you feel like you might be getting handcuffed and shackled to something that may hold you down for the rest of your life? Exit, stage left, right or up, whichever is fastest. Do you have a curious mind and think you might want to pursue a career doing something you love? Yell "fire" and then disappear. Those who become Jehovah's Witnesses as a result of someone knocking on their door have the added disadvantage (or so it seems at the time) of having friends and relationships that are out of alignment with the teaching of their new religion. And so, therefore, have much more to lose than those like myself who were raised in the sect with no exposure to anything else.

The baptism ceremony itself is a fairly low key event. Jehovah's Witnesses do not believe in celebrating personal success or achievements, so the event itself is simple. The ceremony typically begins when those that are to be baptized are led to the front of the auditorium, while usually the front row will be reserved just for them. The speaker will then ask them all a series of questions that must be answered in the affirmative, typically witnessed by thousands in attendance. Once they all have answered these questions in the affirmative, a prayer is given, and the new recruits are led to the pool where they are baptized by getting completely dipped under the water.

The baptism itself is generally performed by certain elders or ministerial servants who have been approved somehow by the local body of elders to perform this dipping process. I happened to be part of the baptismal team one year and had the privilege of working backstage during the actual baptism ceremony. My favorite part was when the women came out in their bathing suits. I had the awesome opportunity to see what they were "working with," and, even though they had strict rules on the type of bathing suit the women could wear, it was still pretty cool getting a "legal" eyeful, all the while, caring for my religious duties during the event.

Once you come up out of the water, you are in. Welcome to the club.

You are now entitled to take the walk of fame. Most of the onlookers are now eating their lunches and socializing with all their friends. So you hurriedly get dressed and make your way through the crowds, much the same as you do in a crowded nightclub. You slap hands with your study conductor and your other new friends. All the rest will congratulate and call you 'brother' or 'sister'. You feel elated. Others will invite you to eat with them, maybe even share some of their food. Yet others will encourage you to their homes for a meal and some good times.

As in the movie, the Matrix, you have swallowed the blue pill.

You are celebrated by your new friends because you have successfully shed all the trappings of the 'world' and have come into an approved standing with God and his spirit-directed organization, so you are told, over and over and over again. At this time, you never think about leaving. The idea of being disfellowshipped for some minor offense never crosses your mind. This organization is perfect, it seems. You are not questioning the many changes in prophecy and doctrine over the many years of their existence. You are not asking yourself if the presence of the governing body is actually scriptural. You are not questioning at this point why Jehovah's Witnesses have a higher than normal suicide and depression rate amongst their young members.

You may not be aware that this organization owns more than a billion dollars of the most desirable real estate in New York. You have not considered for one moment just how judgmental you have become. You have not noticed how little tolerance you have for others' viewpoints, even those of whom you love the most. Have you noticed that the only literary works you read are produced by the WATCHTOWER Bible and Tract Society? Did you know that they are primarily a publishing company? You probably do not know that while they urge their members to pursue ministerial efforts over higher education, many of those that manage the organization hold degrees in law, medicine, and engineering. You heartily embrace the 'truth' that taking a blood transfusion is evil and that you will be harshly disciplined by God if you disobey this. But you have not been faced yet with the prospect of your son, daughter, mother, father or wife dying because of your beliefs about the sanctity of blood.

You are not considering how you will manage if your son, daughter, wife, husband, mother, father or best friend is disfellowshipped, and you can have no more association with them until or unless they return.

You are living in their 'spiritual paradise' now. Critical thinking skills are no longer required. Reading books and exercising your reasoning skills is no longer necessary. No need to form any more opinions based on intelligent thought or to even ponder the future. Your future and thinking have been given to you by the governing body.

This organization seems perfect, that is until you want to leave. And as in the movie, The Matrix, you swallow the red pill.

The red pill represents reality. Just like anything new, the novelty soon wears off when you realize your new found friends are just as prone to having cliques as any other group, society or family. They are just as imperfect, if not more so, as all the church-going people we condemn and judge harshly. A great number of them lie, steal, and cheat just like so many of these horrible 'worldly' people for whom we hold such disdain. To support this, let me tell you a story about two elders in my home congregation in Columbus, Ohio who were wholehearted swindlers and preachers at the same time. Since I cannot be sure whose hands these writings will fall into, I need to change their names. Let's call them Mick and Mack. Mick and Mack both had very nice families and were very well respected in my home congregation. Mick and Mack were average guys without a college education but were somehow doing very well financially in the real estate market. By the eyes of those in the congregation, Mick and Mack were being highly favored by Jehovah because they were being blessed with financial success, and they were being 'used' by God to be a support and pillar to our congregation.

We were so happy to have them. Both had beautiful wives with long wispy hair and curvy shapes that entertained our imaginations during the weekly meetings. The children were equally as beautiful, courteous, and well behaved. Mick and Mack had heavyweight investors that believed in their financial acumen, at least that was the story many of us got.

So, imagine my surprise when my wife and I were watching the news one night, and the headline story was about a local man caught in a real estate flipping scheme. I did not really pay attention until I saw Mick being arrested on live television. Mack would later be arrested the same day with both mug shots plastered across the television for all to see. Could this really be the outstanding elders from our congregation? And it gets worse. Later we would discover that Mick and Mack had financed many homes in the Ohio area for other witnesses with poor credit, cashed out second mortgages, pocketing the money and leaving many of their brothers and sisters in foreclosure and with nowhere to live. To my deep satisfaction, Mick would do every minute of six years in federal prison. Mack who was a childhood friend of mine has been saddled the rest of his life with a criminal record. Mick and Mack would both be disfellowshipped, deservedly so. And how does this story end? Mick ended up with Mack's wife.

You will not hear a story like this when the witnesses come knocking at your door.

During your induction process, you are led to believe that this organization is divinely protected and that Jehovah has direct oversight of those who are assigned to teach and govern. You begin to trust that there could be no "wolves in sheep's clothing" in this organization. The constant dribble from the stage about how God keeps his congregation clean convinces you of this.

So you are incredibly surprised when you hear of sporadic incidents of child abuse in other congregations. You may dismiss this as a result of Jehovah removing his holy spirit from the congregation. But then you hear of a massive lawsuit that was awarded to a certain young woman for the abuse she suffered at the hands of someone in a responsible position in her congregation. Will you dismiss this information too? Curious, you go to the forbidden internet and do a little research on child molestation and sexual abuse and find a myriad of articles and videos detailing one story after another, and the end results are typically all the same. The organization would tell you that these stories are lies developed by apostates to divert you from your faith and your work.

Jehovah protects his loyal servants. How many times have you heard that from the stage with supporting scripture and numerous works published in the WATCHTOWER and AWAKE! Magazines? Do you remember 9/11? I do. I remember exactly where I was when the towers came down killing all those people. Approximately fourteen Witnesses are known to have died in that tragic act of horror. Where was their salvation? According to the organization, Jehovah protects his servants. Had they displeased their heavenly father in some way? Does this unofficial number contain any who were disfellowshipped, or does this particular statistic not include them until or if they are ever reinstated? Herein lies a very fundamental reason why many are attracted to this religion. To observers, this group looks well-protected and peaceful as if there is some invisible wall around them. It is a mirage. Let me illustrate it this way: If you are in a relationship with an abuser who is always telling you that the reason they hit you so often is your fault, that you are bringing it on yourself, what happens? You eventually begin to believe it, and you will try to convince anyone who questions why you stay.

Same with this group. You are continually told that nowhere is there any other peace like the one in this organization, that happiness abounds, and that you serve the 'happy God'; therefore, you should be living joyful lives with joyful people, joyful things, and joyful stuff all over the place. You soon begin to realize that if you want to have friends and a social life, you had better exhibit your joy. So, everyone is demonstrating joy, whether they have it or not. So goes the mirage and so grows the organization.

Do not ignore your curiosity here. Let curiosity run its course. Dig a little deeper. Many witnesses that choose to leave or who are expelled post lots of videos on YouTube. Notice how much pain these people are in? Where does that come from? If this organization is truly blessed as the only channel for salvation, why are these people so angry and hurt? The opposite should be true. They should be admonishing anyone and everyone to stay because there is no other way to salvation. However, quite the contrary is happening. The organization does not stand behind people with critical thinking skills. We all have them to one extent or another. Do their stories have a ring of truth behind them? Think and consider. If your beliefs are strong and based on firm ground and on sound reasoning backed by facts, then you will be able to listen, analyze, and come to your own conclusions objectively.

So, you have swallowed the red pill, and you see the reality. You are not amused. You want out. Now what?

CHAPTER 6

As of this writing, I had suffered through the process of being disfellowshipped three times. I was not outside as a result of some well-planned and executed process. I was unwillingly thrust to the outside. It was this third round that would be my final. I was not going back under any circumstances. I refused to believe the rhetoric I had heard all my life that I would not be able to make it on the outside, that the wicked world would eat me alive, and that I would suffer this unbelievably painful death at Armageddon. I refused to believe that leaving the organization would mean leaving God. I was determined to fight against my every inclination to go back into that high-control atmosphere.

I did not want to go. I had no idea what I would do next, who my friends would be or how to make new friends. I thought I was better than that worldly group of people I was now being thrown to. They were wolves. They were evil people that were surely out to get me. How would I survive this cold evil world? I was being handed over to Satan, and it was going to be a terrible experience. I just knew that all these terrible things would happen to me. Without Jehovah's loving protection over me, my life would fall apart, right? How would I survive the onslaught of evil that will come to me? How would I survive without the daily interactions with my parents and my best friends, the few that I had? My thoughts were out of control. I constantly had the lowest thoughts of myself all the time. My conscience was tormented day and night. Why was I not worth anything to anyone, to God, my parents, this organization to whom I had given my life? What value did my life have? Why was I here? What was I going to do with myself? Who was I?

Fifteen minutes on YouTube and you will see that you (or I) are not the only one overwhelmed with all these feelings after being disfellowshipped from the Jehovah's Witnesses organization or, for that matter, any other religious group that shuns its former members. I doubt these feelings can be totally avoided. I want to discuss with you the coping strategies I used as well as my methodology for growing past the pain and into a successful presence. For any of you that may be reading this material and that are active Witnesses with thoughts of leaving, I want to discuss with you some strategies for quitting, each with their advantages and disadvantages.

The Fade Away

In theory, this method would seem to be the easiest and less painful way to leave the sect. It involves slowly reducing your contact with the organization at all levels. You might do this in a number of ways:

- Lessen the amount of time you spend in the ministry
- Sporadic missing of weekly meetings
- Stop attending yearly conventions and assemblies
- Reducing contact with those in your congregation
- Announce you are changing congregations and then disappear

If you choose this method, you will be seen by the congregation leadership and your friends as spiritually weak, and they will try their best to encourage you to come back into the fold and shore up your spiritual habits so that you can be sure to survive Jehovah's judgments. So, if you decide to continue down this path, it becomes very important for you to develop a convincing story as to why you are not attending the meetings and participating in the ministry as often as they think you should. By the way, as you grow and learn just how much control in your life, you will realize that your reasons for doing what you do are no one else's business but yours. However, in the interim, the fade away may allow you to keep some of your family and friendships intact to a certain level, but you will be eternally harassed about not attending meetings, and it will be difficult to move forward in life to the fullest extent.

Ask yourself this critical question: Do you want to keep the old relationships while you are trying to better yourself and create the life that God truly wants you to live—one not based on fear?

Let me illustrate it this way. Imagine you are married and are having serious problems and doubts about your relationship. You figure that the cost of divorce is simply too high a price to pay. So you move out, find yourself a new lover, and go on with your life. The only thing is, you have not moved on successfully because your spouse has total and complete access to you. Legally, they are still your responsibility, your family, a tie you are bound to. Divorce represents freedom in totality, freedom to live a new life, unbounded to a reasonable extent by the past.

For these reasons, I do not support the 'fade away' as the best method to leave the sect, especially if you are looking to heal and grow into something greater than your current situation. The 'fade away' is not permanent. It is not final. There is no clear line of demarcation. You can be swayed back into the sect by your relationships and the guilt they will place upon you.

Disassociation

This is the willful declaration that you no longer want to be a part of the cult. In general, this requires nothing more than writing a letter to the world headquarters or the local body of elders stating that you no longer want to be one of Jehovah's Witnesses. You will likely be interrogated about your decision and will face a flurry of reasons why you should stay, e.g., that by leaving, you would be risking your relationship with Jehovah and subsequently your life.

If you decide to take this route, you may be tempted to explain your reasons for disassociating, thinking that this might be a time to reason with them about your decision and how you arrived there. They will not be interested in this. I would highly recommend that you decline any efforts the elders might make to meet with you after turning in your letter. Deciding to disassociate yourself is like taking a position of power, quit or be fired. Taking this action is usually not done under duress but after thoughtful consideration and fully understanding the consequences of doing so.

Consequences? What consequences could there possibly be for taking an intentional step to leave an organization that you no longer believe in nor does it meet your spiritual needs? After you have submitted your letter of disassociation, an announcement will be made from the stage stating that you no longer wish to be one of Jehovah's Witnesses. You will now be treated as if you have been disfellowshipped. You will be shunned by your believing family and friends. They will refer to you as an apostate, which is cast in the most negative light.

In my opinion, this method of leaving is preferred because you are leaving willfully from a position of strength. However, doing so must be done with preparation and care. If you are raised as one of Jehovah's Witnesses and have been committed to this organization your whole life and have followed their rules of secluding yourself from others that do not believe like you, then this could potentially be a very lonely journey. If you came into the organization later in life, perhaps as an adult, and you have not totally alienated all your friends and family, your journey may be much easier.

No matter which method you choose, preparation is needed. The reasons that leaving is so difficult have been discussed heavily in this book thus far. Even though I was forced out, recuperating from that has been the hardest struggle of my life. Your sense of belonging to something is gone. I can remember with much clarity being gathered together once per year at the district convention. There could be as many as ten thousand Jehovah's Witnesses attending this event. So there are you sitting in this huge coliseum with thousands of people that believe the same as you. It is very peaceful, people are chatting amongst themselves, families are sitting together, and everyone has a smile on their face. While you are sitting there, someone sitting in front of you, whom you have never seen or spoken too, turns around and introduces themselves to you. Oh, how good it feels to be amongst my brothers and sisters, doesn't it?

So you think to yourself, I must be in that spiritual paradise, right?

You sit back and relax because now you are amongst your brothers and sisters, and soon, awesome spiritual food will flow from the stage decorated with beautiful flowers and security guards. Yes, I said security guards. Why would the speakers need security guards? I always imagined that some heretic would come running down the aisle shouting "Heil Hitler" or something more sinister. Sadly, that would have been a welcome distraction from all the Bible thumping and dribble coming from the stage.

Anyhow, at some point before the program starts, you will be invited to stand up and sing praises to Jehovah. My favorite song was "We Are Jehovah's

Witnesses." While singing that song, the refrain, "We're Jehovah's Witnesses," was repeated so heavily that I now believe it was a method they were using to program our identities. I can recall how I felt when we sang that song, like I was part of this amazing group, it gave me chills. I was proud to be one of Jehovah's Witnesses. That was my life, my vocation, my identity.

And then, it was not.

CHAPTER 7

I was angry. I was pissed off. I was miserable. I was resistant. I was hateful. I had a heart full of venom. I was suicidal. I acted out my insecurities with sex and heavy alcohol use. I spent many mornings recuperating from a night of binge drinking, trying to figure out how to get these two women out of my house and then wondering what sort of disease I may have picked up from my licentious conduct. I had to endure the disapproving stares of my neighbors because they simply could not understand why I preferred to park my car in the front yard instead of in the driveway. I lost my business that I spent several years building. But I can tell you that through all of my careless conduct and self-hate, I never hurt myself and I never caused harm to anyone else. I never spent a night in jail for drunk driving or any other reason.

I often wondered why my reckless conduct did not land me six feet under. Today I understand why. It was not time for me to suffer in this way. I know this sounds cliché, but something higher had a will for me. How many times have we prayed for God to show us what His will is for us, and it felt like no answers were coming? Perhaps God knew that soon it would become evident to many that this was not His organization, that these were not His people, that He was not settling His spirit on just these people alone. Maybe God knew that the governing body was misleading His precious humans. Did God know that their own lies would eventually catch up with them? I think God was preparing me, teaching me how to deal with my own problems and demons created by the organization so that I could help others find a better way to develop their own relationship with their creator.

But it would take years. I would suffer disfellowshipping a total of three times. I was not listening. I was not quiet. The music was turned up too loud. I was listening to the wrong people, the wrong ideas, and the wrong motivations. Little did I realize how much the idea of being created in God's image would later mean to me. Let me explain. As humans created in the image of God, we have the ability to create. So, if God created us and the world around us in His image, then to some extent, we must share the same consciousness, right? Have you ever just sat down quietly with just your thoughts—no music, no television, no internet, no cell phone, and no one in the room with you? Sitting alone quiet with your thoughts can be scary, right? I remember studying tons of WATCHTOWER magazines and hearing a myriad of talks about how bad meditation is for you and that meditating can bring the demons into your mind and life. No doubt, that was one of the most ridiculous teachings ever! When you sit and quiet your mind, this is when God speaks to you. Try this yourself. Take one of your most difficult problems and spend some time with it. Quietly sit and listen to what God whispers to you.

To take it a step further, take any one of the doctrines taught to you by the organization, or any religion for that matter, and just let your mind dwell on it. Do not pray for clarity, do not discuss with others, just sit quietly and let your mind dwell on it. You will be alarmed at how quickly your mind finds all the holes and creates very logical questions against it. You know the truth when you hear it and when you see it. When the weatherman says the rain is coming, you do not sit and try to deny the rain or poke holes in its truth, do you? Of course not. You know it is from a higher source (which may be God for some). It does not cause you pain. It does not make you sad or mad. You know that rain is an expression of love from God, and the Bible clearly states that God is love. So, why in the world would a god that makes stuff and gives things as an expression of love get behind an organization that uses fear as a primary component in its worship?

Listen. Do not be like me. I was disobedient to what God was trying to tell me. So I suffered way more than I had to. Perhaps God put it in the minds of those elders to disfellowship me for a greater purpose. What did I do? I figured my needs were greater than that purpose, so I went back, twice! I can imagine what God may have been thinking. It probably went something like this: "Gee whiz, this guy just doesn't get it. What do I have to do, send this guy a burning bush?"

So, if you are disfellowshipped now, then God has already spoken to you. He has probably been talking to you for a while, but you were unable to listen because the music in your head was up too loud. The last thing you want to do is disregard his counsel and take a course of disobedience.

But what if you are considering disassociation? Where did that idea come from? Was it suggested by one of your 'brothers or sisters'? Did you read it in the WATCHTOWER or AWAKE!? Was it suggested during one of the meeting talks, or did someone message you subliminally?

No. Your God, your creator, spoke to you. What will you do with it? Will you listen? If you choose to listen and heed this communication from God, then I want to help you create your afterlife. What follows is a post analysis of the five steps I took, although not intentional but quite accidental, that led to my healing and have helped me to find peace and success in the life I am now living. Your process may be slightly different, but I do think it will include some or all of the steps we are about to discuss.

The first step, at least for me, was anger. Yes, I was pissed off. I was mad as hell! I was so angry at God that, yes, you could say I hated God and cursed Him on the regular. How could He let me be so misled for so many years? How could He let these people take so much of my youth, my power, and intellect? How could the Almighty God just sit there and let this continue? But was it really God's fault that we did not get out sooner? How long had you had doubts about them really having the truth? How long have you been questioning the changing of doctrines? Unless you were born into the Jehovah's Witness cult, you must ask yourself, was it really God's spirit that led me here or was it something else? The human brain has the highest order of reasoning skills above anything on the earth. You must reckon with the fact that your judgment was faulty, that you fell for the fantasy. Once you do this and restore your faith in your own superior reasoning skills, your anger will subside, and you will start looking for a way to heal yourself.

The second step is the hardest, yet the most critical. For several years, I resisted this vital step. Many of my new friends who saw my struggle and listened to my outcries strongly suggested that I seek out the ear of someone trained to deal with the emotional ups and downs experienced by those who either leave a high-control cult or are forced out. Why is this first step so hard? For me, it was the self-realization that I was not as well as I had thought. I was not as "together" as I appeared to myself and others. I figured that I could make this journey to wellness all on my own. I felt that being disfellowshipped and no longer attending the Kingdom Hall would be enough to affect my well-being positively. However, years of growing up in the Jehovah's Witness faith had created in me a profound sense of self-doubt, insecurity, lack of self-worth, no self-awareness, fear, and an air of superiority over others. None of these traits were going to help me in my quest to move on with my life without having a desire to go back. To move on and make progress, first I needed to address these negative areas.

After leaving a high-control cult, you may be faced with a feeling of deep deficit. You feel that you have lost something of value. In fact, the opposite is true. You may not see it now, but what you are leaving behind is serious negativity and fear mongering. Sharing your thoughts with a therapist will help you realize how fearful you have become. Speaking to a therapist about these matters will not be easy. The first thing you need to understand is that you are not talking to elders, and this is not a judicial committee meeting. Your therapist is not judging you by some imaginary scriptural standard. They are not here to administer retribution for the way you feel or for actions you may have taken in the past. They are here to listen and use their academically trained mind to help you recalculate your self-worth and begin living your life with purpose.

The truth is key. Therapy does not work if you leave your deepest and darkest fears and thoughts unspoken. Therapists and psychologists are trained to deal with the darkest problems and probably have dealt with deeper issues than you and I can ever imagine. So, with that in mind, it is of utmost importance to share everything. Talk directly about how this religion has affected your life. How has it affected your career or lack of one? How about your relationships with your parents, siblings, colleagues, your lover?

How about sexual problems? I had them. My sex life with my wife was the most boring ever! There were things I wanted to do to her, that I wanted her to do to me but feared that somehow the secrets or our love life would come into the open and that made me scared to death. I can remember finding my sexual freedom after divorce, sitting in the Kingdom Hall and looking at all these married couples and just wondering what goes on in their bedroom. All these couples looked miserable. The husbands always looked like they could bust a nut on anything that walked by them, and their wives looked like they had substituted a healthy sexual relationship for chocolate, cakes, chips, and pizza.

I can just see Brother Elder at home begging for a blow job from his wife and her pulling out one of those WATCHTOWER magazines that hinted how bad oral sex was and how displeasing it was to our God. I recall hearing stories of some brothers having oral sex performed on them between return visits or while another brother or sister was conducting a doorstep Bible study.

Sexual dysfunction can be a major factor in ending relationships. God created sex for procreation and enjoyment. If you are not enjoying your sex life with your mate or you suffer from being a bit of a prude as a result of your Jehovah's Witness upbringing, let it out. It will do more good than harm.

Seeing a therapist can also help you to develop a roadmap. For most young people leading ordinary lives, their parents or parent will usually guide them to do things that will help them live successfully. This might include helping them chart a path toward a career, teaching them how to make friends, how to be accepting of others, how to cope with loss, and how to sustain themselves in general. If, however, you were raised in this faith, your parents may not have taught you these fundamental skills. No matter what your age and no matter where you are in life, it is never too late to learn, to rebuild; a good therapist can help you to develop a roadmap to get you where you want to be in your life. Having a detailed roadmap can keep you from focusing on the negativity of the past. It can keep you from feeling like you have fallen behind. Having a strategy with attainable goals can help you to see incremental successes on your road to recovery.

The third step can almost be done in tandem with the second. That is, you must admit to yourself and others that you are lost. You have now resigned from a high-control cultish religious organization that for the most part laid out how you should walk, talk, and think. You will be surprised how many people in your inner circle will respond to you in a very positive way. Now given the fact that you are no longer in the Jehovah's Witness circle of friends, you may be limited to those you work with or even your neighbors. But it is important to share this with someone. Admitting that you are now lost does not mean that you are without direction. It just means that you are now open for discussion about your direction. Admitting you are lost can be the catalyst for discovering what you actually believe. Being open means that you can no longer be judgmental about another person's belief system. Being open does not mean that you accept every thought or idea about spirituality or God that is being thrown at you. Being open means that you hear and consider before dismissing.

Several months ago, I was sitting in my favorite Chicago coffee shop with my computer, writing this story, when a young man walked in. I can recall his rather stately manner, full of confidence and poise. He had an air about himself, a sense of purpose. I took full notice but not enough to catch his attention, or so I thought. As I buried myself into my writing, he ordered his coffee, sat down next to me, and said: "Good morning brother, how are you?" I was accustomed to operating in a closed off state of mind, so it was easy for me to respond with "I'm fine, thanks," and quickly moved on. But this young man had a purpose that simply overcame my resistance. "How has your week been?" he added. At this point, and as if I had no control over my actions, I closed the lid of my laptop and told him I was writing a book detailing my life growing up in a high-control religious cult. I admitted that I had been feeling lost for some time after being disfellowshipped.

That one moment of being 'open' has spurred many deep spiritual conversations with a young but brilliant pastor that has helped me to redefine my relationship with God and use my talents and abilities to help others in the community who are less fortunate than me. That one moment of being open has helped me to see what my purpose is. The act of being open cannot be overstated here. Being open means not being afraid to share. It means not being afraid to admit that maybe, just maybe, the things you were taught were not the truth as you believed them to be. Being open means you must be able to consider other people's viewpoints rationally. People want and desire to help. They may offer you insights from books they have read or even make book recommendations. What you choose to take in should be considered with discernment but considered, nonetheless. For example, during my period of transition, I read a few works that spoke to the questions I had about spirituality, the nature of God, and what we are really doing here on this earth. One of my favorite works is called Communications with God – An uncommon dialogue by Neale Donald Walsh. This book helped me to develop a new perspective on my relationship with God, the value of listening for him and listening to him.

Being in a lost state can be a good thing if we view it that way. Being lost means you are forced to think about your destination and how you will get there.

The fourth step will be one of your most difficult but also one of the most important, and that is to develop a new social circle or network. You will want to be very careful and intentional here. You may be tempted to socialize heavily with other ex-Jehovah's Witnesses, share stories, and talk about all of your bad experiences. This is understandable and may offer you some solace to a limited extent. But remember that those experiences will be mostly negative and could be peppered with a lot of hateful speech and images. Too much of this exposure may cloud your thinking and make it difficult for you to be open to different approaches.

I fell into this very same trap. I feverishly joined a host of Facebook groups, meet-ups, and other venues so that I could share my story and find a place to fit in. However, what I found was a barrage of images and sad stories of lost lives and relationships. While I am sensitive even now to these sad stories, I did not see where too many people were proactively seeking to rebuild their lives. I was reading stories and watching videos of those utterly devastated by the destruction that this organization brings to families and relationships. Many of these people have belonged to these groups and forums for five and ten years, and yet their stories of pain and misery have not changed much over time.

I found myself watching one video after another, reading story after sad story for days on end. What was the result? I could feel my anger boiling for their pain. I could feel my restlessness coming back. I could feel my heart getting heavy again, my focus being diverted. I do not want to negate the benefits these groups can have on people by giving them a place to gather, share, and gain acceptance nor do I want to take away from the moderators who create the content and manage the discussions. These people are providing a much-needed support system. However, it is important to note that *stratospheric growth does not occur when we seek only what is comfortable to us*, when we refuse foreign ideas and concepts, when we do not want to challenge our minds to different perspectives, and when we decline to socialize with those with whom we may have had a disdain for. The process of making new friends and creating new social circles is a process that will never end for you. Think about how excited you were to attend the yearly district convention and the prospect of meeting new people and making new friends. Was it terribly difficult to speak to people? I do not recall having a problem getting people to have a conversation with me. People are naturally inquisitive about others, and we yearn to have social interactions. Nothing has really changed but your social setting. You are no longer one of Jehovah's Witnesses. You no longer are bound by their ridiculous rules which govern social interaction in their world. You are now free to move about the cabin of the world.

Out of all the steps previously outlined, it is this step where I have spent the most of my time in and where I have had the most success with. When I entered this stage of my development, I must admit I felt socially awkward. The same transitions to conversations that I was accustomed to as a Jehovah's Witness which were no longer available to me as they were no longer going to be a part of my new social circle. So it became necessary for me to learn new subject matters with which to engage or simply vary my approach from what I had been taught. Since people love to talk about themselves and their accomplishments, I started asking people not about their belief systems but about them personally. Their personal interests and vocations became of interest to me. Why did they pursue the careers they did? Did they have families, what other places had they lived in, what sorts of experiences had they had? I wanted to learn about their military backgrounds if they had any, and what were their hobbies and interests? I resisted the urge to talk about religion, about God or anything related to spirituality unless they brought it up first, and even then, I was somewhat vague on my background or beliefs. It is important to remember that developing friendships is not a shallow proposition. Developing and creating valuable friendships is not based on the number of field service hours they engage in or in the perceived quality of their presentations or that of a talk they may give from the stage.

Developing new friends is about genuine interest. There are a few books available on the subject of making friends. For example, one of my favorites is a book by Dale Carnegie titled "How to Win Friends and Influence People." Just like anything else in life, success requires preparation. Finding and reading quality books is a sure-fire way to arm yourself with the tools to help you accomplish your goals in developing your new afterlife.

Everywhere you go, at every event you attend, every day at work and in your daily life, you will be presented with opportunities to build upon and extend your network. Do not be afraid to meet those of high social and educational status. You will want to meet and socialize with engineers, lawyers, doctors, business owners, educators, church and spiritual leaders and political figures. These are the very ones that can help lift you up and expose you to new opportunities, help you to develop new ideas and strategies for progressing through to the life you were meant to have.

These are the very ones you held in derision because they chose careers and beliefs different than what you were taught. These are the very ones that will be happy and elated to help you grow once you are honest with them about your time spent under the control of a very abusive cult. They will welcome you to become part of their family. At the end of the day, we all need a support system, and you will find it if you take the time to prepare and search for it.

Irish writer and poet, Oscar Wilde, once said: "Ultimately the bond of all companionship whether in marriage or in friendship is conversation." Go, talk to someone new, and make a friend.

The fifth and final intentional step will by no means be any easier than the previous, and I submit that this will be a step whose conclusion may take a large amount of effort and time before you see significant results. That is you must develop a new belief system. There are many reasons why this will be a challenge. If you came to the cult with a previous belief system, and after leaving, you still believe that God exists, then you must reassess what His will is for you at this moment. It may not be so difficult for you to continue developing your relationship with Him as you did before you became one of Jehovah's Witnesses.

However, if you were born into the cult, your challenge will be greater. I have heard and read many personal accounts where ex-members become atheistic or agnostic in their beliefs. This may or may not be for you, but I challenge you not to be afraid of the unchartered. I challenge you not to be intimidated to attend a church with one of your new found friends. Ask questions and challenge their assertions while being open to allowing them to challenge yours. The important thing is to be open to an array of conversations and opinions. Having these discussions and considering dissenting viewpoints will help you to develop a solid foundation to build your new and truthful relationship with God or for whatever road you choose to travel.

CHAPTER 8

I can recall many discussions about worldly people from the stage as well as during our family studies as if they were some loathsome aliens to be feared and from whom you could only find protection under the roof of the Kingdom Hall. Well, I am very proud to say that I am now a worldly person, and chances are if you are still reading, either you are now a worldly person too or are contemplating this. To all, I say emphatically: "Welcome to the club!" It is a very fun club where freedom of thought, expression, love, and life are not only embraced but also celebrated.

You are now free to think and act as a secular person. Now I know what you are thinking. According to what we were taught as Witnesses, acting like a worldly person with all of their presumed awful indulgences would get us killed at Armageddon. In acting like a worldly person, I am not encouraging licentious conduct or a morally loose lifestyle. I am also not suggesting that your primary interests become those worldly in nature, that you become totally obsessed with things not of a spiritual nature. What I am suggesting is that now life needs to be about balance. For me, a sense of spirituality is needed for I feel a connection to something much larger than myself. However, having this sense of connection also means that I must get to know this world that I was born into. For me, it is important to develop a level of sophistication and experience of some worldly things.

So, for me, life is all about learning. Learning about myself and who I am and what really drives me. My whole life identity has been about being a Jehovah's Witness, and many activities I may have enjoyed as a young person other than theocratic ones were considered worldly and not worthy of much consideration.

For example, when my father became a hardcore Witness when I was about fourteen, I had a myriad of interests in school. I played the drums, the clarinet, I was in the chess club, I was playing junior football, shooting hoops, getting excellent grades, playing in the marching band, and running track after school. Now my mother was a hardcore Witness as well, but she knew how important it was to keep her kids involved in activities that would help them to develop into responsible adults, plus my mom wanted us to enjoy our young lives, and it made her proud when we did well at these things.

However, when my father came in, all those fun things came to an abrupt end. I can recall my mother begging him to let us continue our extracurricular activities because they were beneficial to us. But his response was that the kids at school were worldly and, therefore, bad association. Kudos to my mother. She supported some of our activities in secret, especially when he traveled or was out chasing one of his women across different states. Yes, that's right, you thought Jehovah's Witness men just make devoted husbands and fathers, right? Well, do not ask my mother about that.

So being a newly minted worldly person became for me not about satisfying some depraved, selfish desire but more about self-discovery, and in a few cases, accomplishing some of the things I missed out on as a much younger person. For example, I always enjoyed sports and working out and because I was so involved in trying to meet the rigorous requirements of being a professional Jehovah's Witness, I never really had the time to focus on fitness activities. So for the first time, I recently joined a run club in my new home of Chicago. At first, I was afraid because I knew that I would have to share my life to some extent with these people. People I had never met before, some more educated than me, some better looking than me, some who made more money than me, some no doubt a whole lot smarter than me.

But was I going to let my inner fears defer me from experiencing something great, perhaps reach a long-desired goal such as running a marathon? No, I would not. I took the leap, I joined the club. Each and every week, I prepare and I attend the run club, just like preparing and going to the Kingdom Hall except I was really enjoying it. I was getting mental, emotional, and physical benefits from being a part of this group. To add to this, I was making new friends and being part of a community that was pushing me to get better and succeed.

Initially, my progress was slow and painful, but my forward momentum allowed me to feel confident to complete my first Chicago Marathon in 2014. So, in addition to being a worldly person, I am now a runner and in the best physical shape of my life. This taught me a very valuable lesson. That as a newly minted worldly person, I can be or do whatever I choose to do with my life. So, if you have enjoyed reading this book, you may also add to this that I am now an author as well with several more book titles to come in my future. So, what else can I be? What else can you become as a newly minted worldly person?

When I was in my late teens after high school, I hated going in the ministry for running into my old classmates. When I did, they often wondered why I was going door to door preaching when I should be getting ready for college in the fall. I would offer up the lame teachings that the world would not last long and that they would lose their lives, and I would be victoriously living in the paradise here on the earth, loving the animals, playing with snakes, and burying the carcasses of all the losers like them that chose the wrong side.

However, I secretly wanted to be them. I wanted my parents to tell me that they had planned this wonderful college experience for me where I could go off, develop friendships, study some fancy science discipline like geology, archeology or something similar. But that is not what happened. My "religious" self would not let me pursue my "normal" desires. So, what about my 'worldly' self today? The options are limitless at this point. The real value is that I have placed myself on even playing field with other 'worldly' people when it comes to competing for jobs and entrepreneurial opportunities. By pursuing some of my educational goals, I am now able to have better conversations with people. I feel confident in my abilities to compete effectively and have proven to myself that

I can, again, accomplish anything I want to. I have developed my critical thinking skills which I use in my daily interactions with others who have religious ideals with which I may or may not agree.

I am now in my late forties and feel no limitations on what I can do with my life. All those years spent researching, writing, and delivering amazing talks from the stage that motivated many to clap and sing my praises never earned me a single penny. Today I choose to use my writing skills to educate others and make a living at the same time.

So, who am I now? I am no longer a Jehovah's Witness. I am a 'worldly' person, no longer a follower, blind in a faith. I am an educated man with critical thinking abilities who truly understands that the purpose of fear mongering within man-made structures is designed to keep one's mind in a prison of control. I am a man of faith in myself that has learned the hard way how to listen to the universe when it speaks to me. I am energy and therefore am connected to the universe that is all around me. With this connection comes great power. I will use my ability to build people up and to help them realize the power they have within, their innate power to create, to be amazing and to do powerful works by the very gifts that have been given to me, us, you.

You are now in control. The very next steps you take are entirely within *your* power.

EPILOGUE

So, here we are at the bottom of 2017. Any ex-Jehovah's Witness that is now reading this portion of the book already knows that the struggle never really ends; it only gets easier. This statement accurately reflects where I am even of this writing. The damage, the sadness, never really leaves you when you have children, parents, relatives, and lifelong friends whose lives are still being controlled and ruined by the WATCHTOWER Bible and Tract

Society, the organization behind Jehovah's Witnesses.

For nearly six years now, I have been shunned by my parents and nearly everyone I knew growing up, including my two sons. The year 2014 saw the passing of my grandmother, a devout Jehovah's Witness. I recall visiting with her in the nursing home shortly before she died. Our conversation was rife with musings about the past, my many visits to her house to cut the grass, paint the walls, and all the chores I enjoyed doing around her house. My grandmother had a great memory. I sat near her wheelchair, tears streaming my face realizing that her days had come to a close, clinging to the false hopes of the WATCHTOWER Bible and Tract Society.

She knew. I could tell by the sadness in her eyes that she knew the hope was a lie. I was unable to attend her funeral. The decision to not attend was not an easy one. Being shunned by your family and friends that have given their heart and soul to a group of seven men known to shield pedophiles from the reach of the law, who spew hatred toward those that are not their followers, have evil things to say about those who live alternative lifestyles and refer to those who leave the power of WATCHTOWER mind control as "mentally diseased," can be emotionally draining and heart-wrenching. Knowing that attending the funeral at a Kingdom Hall where I would get no comfort, I elected to stay at home, to safeguard my emotions, to protect the work I had put into righting myself. Instead, I sent a card to my mother offering my condolences. I cried in private and wrote the following in my grandmother's memory and legacy:

Forever in my heart, my dear Grandma Lewis.

Now Grandma Lewis was a funny sort. Drove big cars and rolled with big dogs, and I mean the four-legged kind that bark. Grandma was not a *big baller or shot caller,* but she always had money in her pocket and seemed keen on always giving me a dollar or two as a kid. Between the two grandmas, she was not the most fun to be around. She was strict and was always telling me to go out in the yard and get a switch—again, I do not mean a light switch. I mean one of those switches that were green and flexible yet not hard enough to break.

Grandma Lewis was a sharp lady. She brought style and grace to the wigs of her day. Grandma Lewis made great friends amongst her employers and co-workers. She spent most of her years in domestic services which may explain why visiting grandma Lewis was like visiting an overly sanitized hospital. I can remember how grandma decorated her beds, with lots of bears, dolls, and pillows. She was very particular about those bears, dolls, and pillows, nothing ever out of place.

I remember how my dad would raise me from my slumber on Saturday afternoon because it was time to cut the grass, rake the leaves, and tend the garden at Grandma Lewis's house. Boy, how I hated that yard work! I would mow the grass while trying to ignore the stares of Grandma Lewis's huge German Shepherd. He was always lying in wait, wanting to make my leg his chew toy.

My grandma Lewis loved me, and I knew that. She made sure to call to check up on me wherever life took me. Later, I would visit her at the nursing facility that became her home as she neared the end of her days. She looked up at me from her wheelchair and said: "I know who you are," as she smiled between her loose fitting dentures. "Who am I?" I asked. "You're my number one grandson." Between a gushing of tears, I would spend the rest of that Saturday afternoon rubbing her, kissing her, and loving on her for what would be my last time. I think of her often. What a loss she was to me. *Grandma Lewis, always on my mind, forever in my heart. Rest in peace wherever you may be. You gave me a spark in the ashes of my woes. You gave me the unconditional love that I needed all along.*

Each day that passes finds me doing a little bit better than the day before. I continue to grow in strength and gain comfort in the fact that each and every year thousands are waking up and leaving the control of the WATCHTOWER and beginning the long and painful struggle toward healing. Some are dealing with issues much deeper than the ones I struggle with. Many have broken families as a result. Some have been victims of sexual abuse as children. The power of social media and the Internet will continue to act as a catalyst for exposing the sinister money-making schemes and life-destroying tactics of the WATCHTOWER Bible and Tract Society.

In the depths of my own personal pain, there is hope, there is value, there is help, there is wisdom, there is a resource to be spent helping others find their way. Out of the depths of such pain, a light exists, your future beckons, and you have only to reach for it. I say these words to not only those who are currently living in the Jehovah's Witness or ex-Witness community but to anyone that has been held back and imprisoned by any controlling situation. The way to freedom requires boldness and a willingness to go through the hard times. It will be well worth your effort.

Notes

Steve Hassan, Combating Cult Mind Control (Rochester, VT. Park Street Press, 1998). 5

Resources for further inquiry

Official website of Jehovah's Witnesses:
www.jw.org

Former members' insights:

www.jwfacts.com

www.jwsurvey.org

www.silentlambs.org

Raymond Franz, Crisis of Conscience

(Atlanta, Georgia, Commentary Press, 1983)

Carl O. Johnson, The Gentile Times Reconsidered

(Atlanta, Georgia, Commentary Press, 2004)

Made in the USA
Coppell, TX
17 April 2021